# THE
# S.AILOR,

A

# POEM.

The Authors description of his Youth—Tending Sheep—
Favorite Lamb—Going to Sea—Death of his Sweetheart
—The October Gale in Yarmouth Roads—View of West-
moreland—Keswick Lake and Borrowdale—Trial before
Lord Kenyon—Goes to Sea again—Many remarkable pre-
servations—Dreadful Gale in Torbay - Bay of Biscay —
Taken Prisoner—And after going through various scenes of
Life, returns safe to his Friends who had not heard of him
for several years—Describes Flambro' Head—Burlington
Bay—Yorkshire Wolds—Town and Trade of Liverpool—
The Author's Family with an elegy on his Mother's Death.

## BY EDWARD ANDERSON.

Many Years Master of the Brig Jemima, in the Lisbon Trade.

How charming is variety,
  When with instruction blended ;
Truth drest in neat simplicity,
  Comes doubly recommended.

## LEEDS :

PRINTED FOR THE AUTHOR,
By G. Wilson, No. 3. Kirkgate.
→●◄
Price One Shilling.

**Entered at the Stationer Hall.**

# PREFACE.

*IN an age when literature is arrived at such a pitch of perfection, I am sensible that this little effort of my pen must appear rough and unpolished, to men of a classical and refined taste; and no doubt the admirers of correct style will deem me presumptuous in exposing my production to the critical world. But if it has any sterling value it will be seen by sensible men; they will readily make an allowance, when they are informed, these lines are the effort of uncultivated genius: it is but three years since I first began to write in verse, and the greatest part of this poem was wrote in letters to my friends, \* without any intention of publishing it to the world. As my description of circumstances and places, they knew so well, pleased them, they advised me to improve the talent of poetry. When I remembered the old adage, " Poor as a poet," I saw I had that qualification to begin with. I have known want, and how to abound, and can now say with the poet :*

" Let labour have its due, then peace is mine ;
" And never, never, shall my heart repine."

\* The following is an answer to one of the letters alluded to———

Extract of a letter from Sir Henry Wilson, to the Author.

" Captain Anderson,
" I received the pleasure of your letter yesterday, which gave me great satisfaction to find you in good health and among your friends, who I know, all value and esteem you very much. I never failed to enquire after you, of your friends, whenever I saw them; and from their not having heard from you so long, I found you had been taken prisoner by the French; but I am truly glad you are safe at Kilham, which your description of, and the country you have so long remembered, in your early days, pleased me much—It was natural and manly, and does your heart honour. I think you ought to stay some time at home, and enjoy yourself, as I fear you have gone through many hardships.
" I remain your sincere well wisher,
" Chelsea Park, May 8th, 1804. " H. WILSON."

# THE
# *SAILOR.*

## PART FIRST.

YE muses smile upon a British tar;
  Truth he proposes as his leading star:
He deigns to court you simply, without art,
And offers a rough hand with all his heart,
Since love is often slighted though sincere,
He is content if you but drop a tear;
" Trusting, tho' with you but so few succeed,
" Truth will be heard, and God will bless the deed."
  Ye landsmen listen to the tale I tell,
And sailors, you can understand it well;
Britannia's children listen unto me,
While I describe a sailor's life at sea:
When homeward bound, we cross the raging seas,
With a fair wind, a fine and pleasant breeze;
Below the horizon, as on we steer,
We see the less'ning mountains disappear,
The gale increases, foaming billows rise,
The scud flies swift across the low'ring skies;
The clouds o'ercast the sky—the storm prevails,
And seems to threaten loss of masts and sails,
Altho' we trembling stand at every blast,
High seas arise, yet glad to move so fast:
For as the gale increases more and more,
It wafts us quicker to our native shore.
This cheers us in the dark and stormy night,
When neither moon nor stars do give us light,

Then in our minds pleasing reflections rise,
And thoughts of Friends their absence oft supplies,
A sailor thinks on home, when blowing hard,
When reefing topsails out upon the yard ;
His hands benumb'd, his feet both wet and cold,
The ship she rolls, he scarce can keep his hold
He thinks on her he loves 'bove worldly pelf,
And feels for her as much as for himself,
His loving wife the kindness she has shown,
Thinks on her woes, but smiles upon his own :
When the ship's leaky, or near a lee shore,
He works the pump, exerts himself the more ;
When overboard, this stirs him up to swim,
When he reflects what she must feel for him.
You who have friends that plow the raging main,
Be kind to them when they come home again ;
Disdain them not when they come poor and low.
This is a fact which many people know—
Oft in a common sailor's heart and mind,
Dwell social virtues of no common kind,
Sometimes by friends or fortune cast a float,
They are content when scarcely worth a groat.
Yet scorn by mean servility to please,
Or rise by steps so scandalous as these ;
Low in the world, still they despise its arts,
Tho' nothing else be left but honest hearts ;
They live content, beneath the world's regard,
And bears with ease what seems to landsmen hard :
While I describe what I myself went through,
My brother sailors, I appeal to you :
A leisure hour is all that I can claim,
Your kind applause to me is more than fame.
Let those who can more justly win the bays,

I'll seek my brother's good, and Maker's praise.
  'Tho' I but little education had,
The muses often charm'd me when a lad :
Brought up a shepherd, tho' a farmer's son ;
My clothing then it mostly was home-spun :
My stockings did my mother's taste display,
Black and white wool she mix'd to make them grey.
But then the richest woman in the town
Would go to church in linsey-woolsey gown.
They did not bear the rustic name in vain,
Unpolish'd nature had her ample reign ;
But hardy, healthy, clean, and neat, and spruce,
Content to live upon their own produce.
No need they have of dainty dishes here—
Their sauce is hunger, simple is their cheer.
On Yorkshire Wolds we mostly barley eat,
For there they grew but very little wheat ;
We liv'd on barley bread and barley pies,
And oats and peas the want of wheat supplies :
Bred on coarse fare, this has done me no harm,
My clothes were good enough to keep me warm.

  He who the goodness of his clothes does prize
By their own use, and not by other's eyes ;
If only safe from weather he hast got,
In a small house, but a convenient cot ;
If he, without a sigh or golden wish,
Can eat out of his wooden bowl or dish :
Reader, if in thy mind such greatness be,
The greatest thing's a slave compar'd to thee.

  I little thought that I should plow the deep,
When in Broachdale I kept my father's sheep ;
There I a shepherd's hut and garden had—
There my ambition center'd when a lad ;

With dog, and bag, and bottle by my side,
A shepherd's frock was then my utmost pride ;
I knew no care, but for my father's flock,
Oft watchful eyed my shadow for a clock.
As round my sheep did feed, and lambs did play,
With pleasure then I spent the summer's day ;
Oft basking in the sun I took a nod,
The ground my bed, my head upon a sod ;
My faithful dog he did not go to sleep,
But kept a watch both over me and sheep.
We wisdom may from simple nature gain,
Tho' these are little things which I explain ;
I feel superior to the critic's sneer,
And while I speak the truth I have no fear,
Nor shall the dread but of a paltry scoff,
From what appears my duty beat me off ;
For I am always willing to be thought
A fool, that others wisdom may be taught ;
If God inspire my muse and guide my pen,
I have no cause to fear the face of men.
     What pity fill'd my heart—o'erflow'd my eye—
My father doom'd my favourite lamb to die ;
Commanded me to lift the fatal knife,
But I refus'd—I could not take its life ;
When young, a pet, I fed it on my knee,
And when grown up it often follow'd me.
When I came home, oft met me at the style,
And as I pass'd, play'd round me all the while ;
So fond, it lay all night at the back gate,
Ready to welcome me early or late ;
But I could not prevent the cruel deed,
I wept to see this harmless creature bleed ;
My father smil'd and said, " For shame to cry,

At harvest home the fattest lamb must die."
This dying lamb I could not bear to see,
Puts me in mind of Him that died for me.
I thought this hard, but this was not the worst,
For soon my pleasing prospects all were cross'd,
When fourteen sheep all died in one week,
My hopes were blasted, I'd a trade to seek ;
My parents said, I should tend sheep no more,
They never so unlucky were before.
But still a shepherd's life I most admir'd,
I went to hirings, but could not get hir'd
Without my father's leave ; I tried in vain,
I must come home to husbandry again.
My father said, "Now why should you despair,
"I'll let you go to market and to fair ;
"On a good horse a hunting you shall go,
"And when you money want, then let me know."
Tho' to all these and many feasts I went,
I danc'd and sung, but yet was not content.
A younger brother had left off the plow,
And he was learning navigation too ;
As he was better temper'd far than me,
My mother said, I ought to go to sea.
One night, in anger, Henry let me know,
It was on my account that he must go ;
"When you were shepherd, all things pleasant went,
"But now that you have got the management,
"My home it is no pleasure to me now,
"This is the cause I can't submit to you."
I could not rest, this thought still follow'd me,
If he was drown'd I should unhappy be ;
I staid three days, at nights I could not sleep
So I was forc'd to go and plow the deep.

From all my fond connections doom'd to part,
To leave them then, it almost broke my heart,
On Wandle Hill I view'd the distant deep,
Look'd back and wept, and stopp'd again to weep.
　The port of Scarbro' is well known to me,
That was the the place where I first went to sea.
Jacket and trowsers there I first put on,
And all that saw me laugh'd at country John ;
There to a friend I gave my country coat,
Took up my bed, and went into the boat;
O how I trembled when I left the shore !
I never had been in a boat before ;
The boat was small, they bade me lay me down,
I heard them say that we should all be drown'd ;
I thought my troubles soon would all be done,
But since, I found that they were just begun.
I could not swim, so I had little hope ;
At length we reach'd the ship, they threw a rope,
Sick and half drown'd they haul'd me up the side,
The ship she had beat out to sea that tide.
　When first I heard them cry out, *topsail haul*,
I thought the masts upon my head would fall,
Tho' sick and faint, some pleasure I did find
When we began to sail before the wind ;
It fell less wind, more smooth along the shore,
My fears were fled, my sickness soon was o'er ;
A pleasant breeze, and a fine moonlight night,
Then I began to whistle with delight ;
The mate he heard, and soon call'd out to me,
" You must not whistle when you are at sea,
" Remember now you are not tending sheep,
" We only whistle when the wind's asleep."
The Portuguese just as much wisdom show,

When calm they cry, *Blow, St. Anthony, Blow,*
Much superstition I have seen since then,
And silly customs amongst different men.
The men look'd out before, the mate abaft,
At eight o'clock he call'd, *All hands come aft,*
Then they divided us with quick dispatch,
Call'd one, The larboard, one, The starboard watch :
It prov'd my turn in the first watch below,
I did go down, to sleep I could not go ;
Disturb'd by foaming waves and whistling wind,
And thinking on the joys I left behind ;
Rock'd in my hammock as she rolling goes,
Just before twelve I fell into a doze :
Alarm'd when I had nearly fall'n asleep,
I dream'd that I was sinking in the deep ;
Lord save, I cried, I am not fit to die—
Just then I heard a dreadful midnight cry,
They stamp'd on deck, which made all ring below,
And one cried out aloud, *Starboard watch, hoa !*
A larm'd and terrified, it made me jump,
This awful noise did sound like the last trump ;
My guilty conscience magnified the sound,
I wak'd rejoicing that I was not drown'd.
Since then how many dangers I've gone through,
I well may wonder I've escap'd till now ;
The wind still fair, a fine and pleasant night,
We made a light-a-head, 'twas Tynemouth light ;
Then we hove too, off Suter Point we lay,
And waited tide until the break of day :
The morn arose, and smoky Shields appear'd,
All hands made sail, and for the bar we steer'd,
New scenes arose as day light spread abroad,
A boat came off the pilot came on board ;

" Pull off your jackets, boys, now bear a hand,
" Let some good sailors by the braces stand."
Then he came forward, said to me with scorn,
" This country hobuck, where has he been born ?"
The girls on shore, in their Newcastle brogue,
They call'd me Country Lumper, Yorkshire Rogue ;
When I was look'd upon with such disdain,
I wish'd I had been tending sheep again.

   Reluctant, from each fond connection torn,
What hardships on the ocean I have borne !
Tho' oft severe, yet they quite light did prove
To what I suffer'd from the effects of love.
This tender passion soon an object finds,
And close united by congenial minds.
But ah ! before the sacred knot was tied,
Death came and snatch'd away my promis'd bride,
When bound to sea, then home with her I went,
In love and innocence the night we spent ;
I talk'd of my return, the joys how sweet,
She wept and said, we never more should meet.
Although our parents both of us did blame,
We could not part before the morning came.
I call'd next day to bid a last adieu,
And of her charms to take another view ;
Her look shew'd kind affection, love sincere,
I turn'd away to hide the falling tear.
We social pleasures must no longer share,
Doom'd to the sea, the ship must be my care;
To plow the deep where waves do rage and foam,
ar from my friends, my family and home.*

* The change from the retired life of a shepherd to that of the toils and
perils of the foaming ocean, cannot be fully described, his habitation is not
fixed : rolling from side to side ; tost about by every breath of wind, and bois-
terous waves ; often for months he does not behold the cheerful face of wo-
man ; at night he slumbers in a narrow hammock, from which amidst dreams

Next news I heard from home when far remote,
And by my brother Henry it was wrote,
Informing me our family were well,
But of her death he seem'd quite loath to tell.
At last, "Dear brother, now prepare your mind,
"For reading that which still is left behind;
"When you left home we thought it was not right,
"We blam'd you much for stopping out at night :
"It seem'd unkind from us to run away,
"That the last night at home you would not stay.
"Miss Blanchard, she more pleasing was to you,
"Her beauty captivating I allow ;
"None had objections to her for your wife ;
"Her health and strength were promising long life,
"All shew'd a prospect fair of worldly bliss,
"But now alas ! how soon 'tis come to this ;
"This night a corpse—no more her voice is heard
"To-morrow she must lie in the church yard ?
"Where are the joys her beauty could afford ?
"Dear brother, now prepare to meet thy God."
    For many years I far abroad did roam,
Still I remember'd her when I came home.
This all the satisfaction I could have,
To drop a silent tear upon her grave.
Ye loveliest of her fair survivors, see

of home, he is often roused by scenes of danger; rushing on deck, he finds
the vessel laid upon her side by a sudden squall. Perhaps the rest of the night
is spent amidst cold, and wet, and darkness, and storms ; and at the morning
light no green fields or cottages are to be seen ; nothing but a turbulent and
boundless ocean, in which he may possibly soon be overwhelmed. But storms
do not always vex the surface of the deep ; favourable breezes at intervals drive
him swiftly along. Then he can say, How pleasant is the life of a sailor ! he
enjoys that pleasing variety which Epicureans often seek in vain; the fruits,
the productions, the manners of distant climates, are all familiar to him. He
sees nature under every aspect ; and the widely varied faces of mankind: the
Indian and the Negro, the Russian and the Turk, are brothers with whom he
has frequently conversed.
    He sees the sun rise in all its glory, and disappear in the evening as in a
sea of fire ; he alone, with his level horizon, can contemplate, in all its magnifi-
cence, the star-light canopy of heaven, or the moon reflected on a thousand
broken waves. Who would not undergo a few hardships to arrive at the enjoy-
ments of objects so sublime ?

What weak defence from death your charms can be,
O how the Lord has hedg'd about my way,
And often robb'd my passions of their prey,
In love withheld my every fond delight,
And kindly starv'd my grov'ling appetite :
May all my life shew forth his love and praise,
For all the mercies of my lengthen'd days.

I was preserv'd upon the raging main,
In the West Indies from a hurricane :
I saw the goodness of the Lord most clear,
When in the Juno * we dismasted were ;
The ship a wreck, but still she did not sink,
At short allowance both of meat and drink.
When toss'd about for thirteen weeks or more,
At last we all but one got safe on shore.
Again preserv'd, I saw the hand divine,
In the October gale, in eighty-nine.
More than a thousand men were lost that day,
When in the Friendship ‡ I was cast away :
A passenger from London I came down ;
In Yarmouth Roads we lay, to Hull were bound ;
Of this large fleet, there hundred ships or more,
One hundred sail were lost, or drove on shore.
The night was moonlight, weather very fine,
Our women passengers were eight or nine,
They sung us songs in which we took delight,
Some play'd at cards till twelve o'clock at night,
And when I went to bed, long musing lay,
Thinking how to divert them the next day ;
Hearing a noise before the storm came on,
I wak'd, and all my pleasing dreams were gone.
In vain I try, for language it must fail
To give account of this destructive gale.

* Juno, Capt. Resom, of Portsmouth, Virginia.
‡ Friendship, Capt. Stevenson, Hull Cutter,

At night 'twas calm, quite smooth, and still the main,
The morning ushers in a hurricane :
At four o'clock this dreadful storm did rise,
An awful darkness veils the lofty skies ;
The waves were foaming, loud the billows roar,
And dash tremendous on the trembling shore.
All hands were ca'l'd, quick on the deck they run,
We scarce could muster ere the gale begun ;
Then all employ'd, each to their station go,
Most up aloft, but some must stay below ;
To pay out cable, and to keep it clear,
Likewise to mind she did not break her shear ;
To hand main-top-sail then we made a shift,
But, found, when we came down, the ship adrift:
When veering out, too rash the captain spoke,
To bring her up, and then the cable broke ;
Altho' we let another anchor go,
We drove on board another ship we saw,
Which struck our quarter, stove in all abaft,
Likewise companion broke main boom and gaft.
How to get clear it all our art defies,
We heard the women's dreadful shrieks and cries.
We hail'd the other ship, they could not hear,
Their captain tried to get his vessel clear :
He vear'd out cable, this was death to him,
It tore him round the windlass limb from limb ;
O what confusion, terror and dismay !
Then we got clear, and sheer'd the other way ;
Our anchor held, and we brought up agair,
But 'twas not long that there we could remain.
I went below the passengers to cheer,
And just had told them that they need not fear,
I heard them cry on deck, " Now save us Lord,

"Another ship is coming straight on board."
I started up, two women held me fast,
By using force I got away at last;
Their frantic looks shewd terror and dismay,
But looking round, I saw two children play;
The oldest, as he roll'd from side to side,
Cried, Mother look how finely here I ride;
They seem'd to wonder what we had to fear,
The youngest cried aloud, Mamma look here.
By tender looks distinguish'd from the rest,
She clasp'd the smiling infant to her breast.
And as the mother gave the child a kiss,
The baby lisp'd, Mamma, what noise is this?
I thought I should not fear the raging seas,
If I was but as innocent as these.
I heard a woman calling out to me,
I turn'd and saw the bible on her knee;
Her looks then shew'd that she was quite resign'd
But other souls she bore upon her mind;
Warn them on deck, she said, to be prepar'd,
And pray to God that we may all be spar'd.
Then all stood waiting our impending fate,
We cut the cable but it prov'd too late;
Against our bow she came with such a sweep,
Ship and all hands they sunk into the deep.
Whilst I ran forward to get our ship wore,
Abaft they had agreed to run on shore;
Afraid of that because I could not swim,
The captain sick, in vain we call'd on him,
I took the helm, and kept her off the shore,
For there I thought the danger it was more.
We seem'd each moment still on ruin's brink,
They all supposed that she soon must sink.

Some went to prayer, and on their knees did fall,
And some cried out that I should drown them all,
One hove the lead, the mate look'd out before,
We kept her in three fathoms near the shore ;
Seas breaking o'er us, dark, we could not see,
Of other ships we ran on board of three.
It seem'd a miracle that we got clear,
We kept afloat till day-light did appear ;
I thought, while thousands view'd us from the shore,
Were I safe there, I'd go to sea no more;
I promis'd then if God would spare my life,
To quit my sins, and lead a better life;
If sav'd, that I would give to God the praise,
And serve him truly all my lengthen'd days.
But how ungrateful I have been since then,
In that respect I was the worst of men.
The men cried out a-head they saw a wreck,
Five men were floating on a quarter deck,
Driving before the wind, the sea and tide,
Thus tost about, sometimes the sea did hide;
Their station dreadful, thundering billows roar,
And what a distance from the long'd-for shore !
No refuge but in God, unless he please
They must be lost amidst the raging seas.
As o'er the Stamford we our course did steer,
O what a dreadful scene did there appear.
So many wrecks that clear we could not keep
Around us sailors sinking in the deep.
We saw on the Homeheads * a vessel lie,
The crew wash'd from the rigging, sink and die ;
On Lowestoffe Point, beheld a sloop on shore,
Fell off and fill'd, we saw the crew no more,

* Homeheads, a sand-bank.

Another wreck we saw in the South Road,
They cried for help, but none could get on board ;
None could assist them as no boat could live,
God only then effectual aid could give.
Friends weep for him who on a death-bed lies,
They cannot save his life—he faints and dies.
Just so with them, men view them from the shore,
All they could do was pity and deplore,
After we had got out thro' all these wrecks,
Then we began to try to stop the leaks ;
No gaff, nor boom, nor anchors then we had,
And still we thought indeed our case was bad.
Before the gale we drove along the shore,
The leaks began to gain upon us more,
The ship a wreck, no harbour could we reach,
So all agreed to run her on the beach.
As near to Harwich, then we did advance,
Under Red Cliff, we thought it the best chance ;
We haul'd her in close up to the Pie Sand,
The sea more smooth beneath this point of land ;
The tide it then was quarter ebb or more,
To save our lives we ran the ship on shore ;
On the ebb tide the heavy seas did stand,
But at low water we got safe to land,
The women almost dead while on the main,
On shore they all but one reviv'd again.
 Can I forget, unto my latest breath,
How narrowly I then escap'd from death ;
When hundreds round me met a watery grave ?
O what a grateful heart I ought to have ?
When looking on the corpse that wash'd on shore,
I promis'd to offend my God no more ;
But while I mix'd with pleasure-taking crowds,

My goodness it was like the morning clouds,
When safe on shore, I purpos'd there to keep,
Determin'd never more to plow the deep;
For still a country life I most admir'd,
And into Westmoreland I then retir'd:
There safe from busy crowds, and war's alarms,
Where the pure country spreads unclouded charms:
The fertile plains, the lakes, the hills, the trees,
The fancy strike, the eye with rapture sees;
What awful thoughts did in my mind prevail,
While viewing Keswick Lake and Borrowdale;
Struck with surprise, when first those scenes I saw,
It seem'd just like a paradise below.
Looking around with admiration still,
I saw a cloud just climbing up the hill;
The scene soon changes as I upward look,
The tops of hills were all seen wrapt in smoke;
As I went up along the mountain side,
There a romantic prospect open'd wide:
But when I came upon the top so high,
There I seem'd plac'd between the clouds and sky;
The mist had drawn a veil o'er herds and flocks,
And nothing could be seen but tops of rocks:
I seem'd like Noah, escap'd from the deluge,
The ark on such a mountain took refuge;
This something like that awful scene did show,
When he look'd down upon the world below;
My mind was lifted up, and like the dove,
I could find nought to rest on but above,
A rainbow shew'd, as it began to clear;
A deep abyss, the vale did then appear:
But when the sun broke out upon the plain,
Then it seem'd like a paradise again;

It beams a variegated scene display'd,
Spreading along alternate light and shade ;
What different hues amongst the trees were seen,
Of dark and light, brown, yellow, red, and green.
As I sat there, upon the mountains brow,
And view'd the dales that lay so far below ;
The awful precipices made me fear
Of hastily approaching them to near :
Their form in many places is so steep,
A man would be in danger tho' he creep.
The distant mountains rise prodigious high,
Their pointed tops they seem to touch the sky ;
These mountain tops are strew'd with ragged rocks,
With here and there some heath, and scattered flocks
A few small sheep of an inferior kind,
But bound by lordships, not in fields confin'd :
As on these hills the cultivating hand
Has done but little to improve the land ;
And here the mountains much the same appears,
As we presume, for many hundred years ;
And on their surface little more is found
Except moor-fowls ; and other game abound :
Their produce slate, and peat for fuel made,
For which but little more than labour's paid.
But in the dales, altho' so deep they run,
As sometimes nearly to exclude the sun ;
Yet fertile fields, both corn and pasture fair,
We see abound in many places there.
In these grotesque recesses men reside,
As far from cities as their wealth and pride :
In language, manners, houses, diet, dress,
Originality they all possess :
Amongst them true simplicity we find.

To strangers always courteous aud kind :
Of late they learn refinement with such speed,
Some learn to dance before they learn to read.
Pleasing society I soon did find,
And this romantic country charm'd my mind :
Tho' poor, yet I enjoy'd content and health,
Careless of honour, grandeur, fame or wealth.
But Providence did soon my plan defeat,
A summons brought me out from this retreat ;
Hurry'd to London from those silent bow'rs,
By the mail coach, in eight and forty hours,
A witness on a trial to attend ;
To all my former schemes this put an end,
A ship I had been mate of brought me forth,
Being insur'd for more than she was worth ;
The captain wish'd to run the ship on shore ;
This he attempted several times before :
When none of us would to his terms agree,
The rudder he unshipp'd in the East Sea,
When we all saw the scheme that he had plann'd,
The crew prevail'd on me to take command,
Seeing the danger all were sore afraid,
But we a temporary rudder made,
'Twas in November, off Bontholm we lay,
Long stormy nights, and short the winter's day ;
Tho' toss'd about by the strong furious blast ;
To Copenhagen we got safe at last ;
There the long winter eighty-eight we lay,
And were froze up until the third of May,
Tho' far from home, the winter cold severe,
Yet glad to find a friendly shelter there.
    When I before lord Kenyon trembling stood,
Could I expect that it would work for good ?

My friends, my character, were all at stake,
I sacrific'd them all for conscience sake ;
And prov'd this true—tho' they are falsely blam'd;
Who speak the truth, need never be asham'd,
Counsellor Erskine said to me, " Take care,
You in the presence of his lordship are."
I said, " I stand before the Lord I know,
" My cause is good, I fear no lord below ;
" Nor do I fear this day the truth to prove,
" Both in the sight of men, and God above."
This was a cause that had before been try'd,
But three false witnesses the truth did hide :
Altho' they all again the same did swear,
By what I said, the truth did plain appear ;
And I was then promoted on that ground,
They thought an honest Yorkshire man was found
And, by the underwriters, Master made,
Of the Jemima, in the Lisbon trade,
This prospect, both of pleasure and much gain,
It tempted me to go to sea again,
From low degree, this trial did me call,
From threshing in a barn at Hornby Hall. †
I saw the hand of God that did me raise,
But then I did not give to God the praise :
Prosperity did such a charm afford,
That I soon turn'd away from serving God.
A brother call'd upon me twice or thrice,
Reprov'd me freely, gave me good advice ;
" Tho' captain now, and worth a little pelf,
" I know you still, but you forget yourself ;

† Near Appleby, in Westmoreland.

" When ye go home, 'twill make the neighbour's stare,
" To see you wearing powder in your hair :
" At home plain Edward, once we did you call;
" Don't be too proud, your pride may have a fall."
His words prov'd true, they were not spoke in vain,
Plain Edward he has heard me call'd again.‡
What tho' prosperity some pleasure brings,
Yet how uncertain are all earthly things :
This truth to me hath oft been clearly shown ;
Once when I had a vessel of my own,
Coming from Lisbon laden with fruit and wine,
Our passage short, the weather very fine ;
Passing the Cape, across the bay to steer,
There we fell in with a French privateer :
Old captain Vining then with us had sail'd,
And to keep company we had not fail'd.
As they at day-light did with glasses look,
Suppos'd that he was English by the smoke ;
They pass'd by us, and straight for him they stood,
For he was burning coals, but we burn'd wood.

‡ Extract of a letter from Henry Anderson, dated Dover, August 10th, 1795.
" Dear Brother Edward,
" I am highly pleased to hear that you have had such a ready voyage and
safe return ; I called at Deal about a fortnight ago, and Miss Errige informed
me that she had received a letter from Miss Emmerson, on the preceeding day,
and she expected you in a few days. From your last I find you did not get
home in your voyage to the North ; but I expect you will perform what you
promised (your life being spared) of going to see our aged parents and other re-
lations, I would advise you to go not as a person to be admired for your cloth-
ing or fashionable dress, or that you can ride in a coach to your father's house,
but that you may be humble and lowly in heart like a wise man. I hope you
will not discover the vanity of the human heart, in thinking money should
command attention, in making us wiser or more happy ; you may have things
descent, but cut off all superfluity. Let them know in Kilham, that wisdom,
not folly is the object of your pursuit. I would have you remember that the
time was when you were called Ned and plain Edward, afterwards Mr. and now
Captain Anderson, but such appellations do not alter our state as it relates to
God and Eternity. I see no necessity for you to wear hair-powder; make no
excuses for pride, let it be execrated and detested by us all. God resisteth the
proud, but exalteth the humble and meet.—Read Daniel, chap. iv. verse 28.
When you go home let some be benefited by your benevolence and good ex-
ample. I have much to say, take these few hints as a specimen of the rest.
" I remain your loving brother till death.
" HENRY ANDERSON,

They next pull'd to a Swede, 'twas calm all day,
At night it came a breeze, we got away;
The packet ta'en by which my letters went,
Which sav'd insurance then eighteen per cent,
This news amongst the merchants welcome sounds,
Jemima—Anderson's safe in the Downs.
When through the Narrows we made our way.
And beating up upon the flats that day;
To gain the Nore that tide we did our best;
But it came on a gale at West North West,
I thought none happier than myself that day,
A blast of wind soon blew it all away;
Thinking next day I should my sweetheart see,
Among my friends, how welcome I should be:
The gale came on so sudden and so hot,
Sweetheart and friends, they soon were all forgot.
Be quick, haul up the main-sails in the brails,
Run down the jib, clue up top-gallant-sails,
The sudden quall, it laid her down so low,
To bring her up, we let the anchor go;
When no abatement of the gale we found,
And at low water we should be aground;
Night coming on the danger there to shun,
We cut the cable, through the Narrows run,
And anchor'd in the Gore, the buoy is white,
But parted from our cable in the night.
Adrift, no anchors, what was best to do,
A cadge and hawser then we did let go;
When we had drifted far, and near the shore,
It caught a rock, and brought us up once more;
Altho' the sea ran high, the ground not clear,
Yet it held fast till day-light did appear.
Just to the West of Margate then we were,

A boat came off, and run us safe in there ;
They ventur'd off, altho' it blew so hard,
And got a hundred pounds for their reward.
Tho' death appear'd that night on ev'ry side,
A harbour safe the Lord did there provide.
   Preserv'd again, I did his goodness see,
On Christmas eve, the year of ninety-three,
When riding in Torbay, the wind at West,
But it came on a gale at East South East ;
Tho' some their cables cut, their sails did spread,
Yet many could not weather Berry Head.
We dropp'd both anchors, we could do no more,
But drove amongst the breakers near the shore :
Just before dark, two ships on shore were cast,
And five or six we saw without a mast.
All round us flying signals of distress,
Night coming on, the gale did much increase ;
The wind we heard it whistling in the blocks,
And the high surges beating 'gainst the rocks ;
Nothing but death appear'd before our eyes,
A ship drove past, we heard their dreadful cries ;
On rocks to pieces dash'd, an awful sight,
Soon all was cover'd by the veil of night.
While men on shore their Christmas gambols play,
We stood expecting to be cast away ;
Nor mind the wet and cold, tho' 'twas severe,
We only thought upon the rocks so near.
The wind came suddenly about once more,
To the North East, and that was off the shore ;
In our behalf, when we were most afraid,
We saw the goodness of the Lord display'd.
We taste the sweets of pleasure after pain,
Joy warm'd my heart, like sunshine after rain.

C

Preserv'd again, it was the will of heaven,
From sinking, in the year of ninety seven,
To Lisbon bound, our convoy the Sea Horse;
In a hard gale we all the fleet did lose;
Left in distress, when we were half seas o'er,
Could I expect to see my native shore;
The leak still gaining, boats wash'd off the deck,
We threw the cargo out to stop the leak ;
Still it pour'd in—the boats gone over board,
And nothing left to trust in but the Lord ;
We cry'd to him who then beheld our grief,
And soon he sent a ship to our relief.
May seamen learn from shipwrecks, winds and storms,
To fear that God who all his will performs ;
That God, whose providence marks all our ways,
And at a glance surveys our future days,
The best concerted schemes that men have plann'd
Prove vain, if not supported by his hand.
  Tho' unto Lisbon I had often run,
Without a couvoy, since the war begun ;
When I with convoy 'mongst the fleet did steer,
Then I was taken by the privateer,
Which in disguise surpriz'd us in the night,
And before day light run us out of sight ;
And other three into their hands did fall.
Our convoy was the Argo, captain Hall.
When ta'en again, tho' sore against my will,
Then I was forc'd to sign a ransom bill ;
To save myself and crew from being drown'd,
Incurr'd a penalty of five hundred pound,
They had agreed our ship should be restor'd,
And had put all their prisoners on board ;
Then it fell calm while they did us detain,

And they came back to plunder us again ;*
The wine and die-wood which was stow'd below,
Were taking out, then meant to let us go ;
Left without boat or ballast we must be,
Except I would unto their terms agree ;
And this had put our people in such fear,
That two had enter'd in the privateer.
I saw the crime, but looking at the cause,
My feelings stronger were, than human laws:
Then they left us a boat, our lives to save,
For ballast, empty water casks they gave,
One then on board, a witness to this scene,
Was captain Williamson, of Aberdeen;
When to the Adm'rality I did apply,
Then they advis'd a counsellor to try ;
When I consulted with Sir William Scott, †

* Extract from the Protest.

The brig Jemima, Edward Anderson master, sailed from Lisbon on the 10th of May, 1797, under the convoy of the Argo, Captain Hall, and two other ships of war: on the twenty-second of the same month, before daylight in the morning, she was captured by the La Neptune, a French privateer, who took her away out of the fleet. But at day light in the morning, seeing some of the fleet in sight, and one ship coming towards them, they left the Jemima taking with them all the fire-arms, papers, and part of the captain's clothes.— That at 8 o'clock the same morning, she was again captured by the La Minerve, another French privateer, who began to take out the Jemima's cargo, and carried it on board the privateer, they put all the English prisoners on board the Jemima, and still continued taking out the cargo. Captain Williamson and several of the people went on board the privateer, fearing to remain in the Jemima, as the Frenchmen had taken her boats, quadrants, provision, &c. and she was like to be left in a dangerous state for want of ballast. The captain of the privateer would not permit any Englishman, to remain on board of her, except they would enter into his service, Capt. Williamson's mate and another man did enter, chusing rather to run the risk of their lives by fighting against their country, than to remain in the Jemima, Capt. Williamson was sent back on board the Jemima, and desired to acquaint Capt. Anderson that if he would ransom the vessel for 200 guineas, they would take no more of the cargo out. When Captains Anderson and Williamson, with the rest of the crew, consulted together, they were all of opinion, that to ransom the vessel was the only means of saving their lives; in consequence of the danger, Capt. Anderson agreed to the ransom, and his mate was willing to go as hostage; the French captain then gave them according to agreement, a boat, and some empty water casks to fill for ballast, and then left them; and by God's providence they arrived safe in London.

† Capt. Anderson's consultation with Sir William Scott,

Question—Is the cargo on board liable to pay the ransom or expences attending to the hostage ?

Answer—No part of it.

He could give no relief—pity'd my lot :
My case was hard, but laws are so exact,
He could find no exception in the act.*
" Those troubles oft are sent to make us wise,
" Afflictions oft are blessings in disguise ;
" And pain we see in pity oft is sent ;
" Oft we're chastis'd to bring us to repent."
Then I left all my friends, and native shore,
Fully determin'd to return no more,
In foreign parts I purpos'd to remain,
But was against my will brought back again;
 May holy flame divine, and heav'nly fire,
My simple muse with sacred warmth inspire :
Suggest each thought thy glorious ways to trace ;
And tell the wonders of redeeming grace.
" I once seem'd happy, had the world's good word,
" And with it ev'ry joy it could afford ;
" Friendship and love seem'd tenderly at strife,
" Which most should sweeten my untroubled life,
 " Flatter'd where'er I went amongst the fair,
"I laugh'd and trifl'd, always welcome there ;
" But yet true happiness I could not find,
" Riches could never ease my troubled mind ;
" My conscience still perform'd her proper part,
" And wrote a doomsday sentence on my heart."
 Passions indulg'd, fill'd me with guilty fears,
And my soft pillow oft was wet with tears.

*Question*—What steps will be most proper for Capt. Anderson to take to release the hostage, and what steps in general would you have him to take in this business ?

*Answer*—I have seen and consulted the several papers, and am clearly of opinion, that under the terms of the act of parliament, this contract is nul and void, and is incapable of being supported in any court: but under the special circumstances of the case, I think there is a strong call on the humanity of the owners of both ship and cargo. *Wm. Scott.*
 2nd May, 1797.

*The act of parliament alluded to, intitled, "An Act to prevent Ransoms," expresses, "That if any master, or owner shall ransom his vessel, he shall be liable to the penalty of Five Hundred Pounds."

" Hard task for me who lately knew no care,
" And harder still, as learn'd beneath despair;
" My hour's no longer pass'd unmark'd away,
" A dark importance sadden'd every day,
" God's holy word, once trifling in my view,
" Now by the voice of my experience true;
" Tir'd of the world, I went from place to place;
" Sin, death, and hell, oft star'd me in the face;
" Against these fears how often did I spurn:
" And yet conviction would again return,
" If sudden Death was mention'd, then thought I
" What will become of me if I should die;
" Sinners who see no danger in their state,
" Perhaps they may, perhaps they may too late;
" But when the sound of pardon pierc'd my ear,
" I dropp'd at once my fetters and my fear."
And now I call my readers to employ,
A few short hours in list'ning to my joy,
   As in a Dublin trader then I sail'd,
'Tho' I shun'd sin, temptation oft prevail'd;
I'd left my family for sev'ral years,
Till one of them in Liverpool appears;
It seem'd that nothing to my heart could reach,
While there I heard my brother Henry preach:
I did not know 'twas him when he begun;
He said, " The father had another son ;
" This son he had in a far country been.
" And many scenes of hardship he had seen ;
" Forsaking, and forsaken by all friends,
" Then he perceiv'd where earthly pleasures ends;
" But there he did his sins and folly mourn,
" And said, he to his father would return."
Altho' he did not know to me spoke,

It was apply'd; my heart was almost broke,
He preach'd one Sunday, at Mount Pleasant Hill,
I went to hear but did not know him still;
But as I went on board when he had done,
I heard them say, his name was Anderson;
I soon found out that it must be the same,
He came from Kilha..., Henry was his name;
To own him then my pride did me prevent,
Conscience accus'd me, but to sea I went.
I told this to a friend I went to see,
And she was more affected far than me:
Thoughts of a brother made her burst in tears,
Of whom she had not heard for many years:
When I in her such tenderness did see,
'Twas then I thought how hard my heart must be:
" I have a mother and a sister too,"
She said, " feel for t hem : you must write now."
By her pursuaded, I could not refrain,
Their friendly answers * brought me home again?

*Extract of a Letter from Henry Anderson, dated Liverpool, 29th of Nov. 1807.*

" Dear Brother Edward,
  " Your letter with its most interesting contents, came safe to me
yesterday, when I had just finished the forenoon preaching; from the direction
you had put on it, I could not conceive from whence it had come, I therefore
immediately on opening it, looked for a name, and when I saw your's sub-
scribed, I cannot express the surprise and joy which I felt on your account;
Joseph's brethren could not be more affected with the surprise they felt, when
he made himself known to them; or old Jacob when he saw the waggons, sent
by Joseph to fetch him into Egypt, he cried out, 'Joseph is yet alive! I will
go down to see him before I die.' I felt and better understood what our Lord
intended to convey unto men in the parables of the prodigal son, the lost sheep,
and the pieces of silver; the father had another son, and he justified his joy a-
gainst the murmers of his eldest son, by saying, 'This, my son, was dead and
is alive again : was lost, but now is found.' Now, although I have other bro-
thers, of whom I have heard, and whom I have seen, yet to hear of you, who
have been so long as one lost to the family, I felt peculiar emotions exulting in
my heart. I have had many thoughts about you within this month or five
weeks since, a stranger called at Pit-street chapel one Wednesday night, and
asked the keeper of the chapel if one of the name of Anderson preached there :
he asked my other name, identified my person, stature, hair, complexion, &c.
and asked if I were not a Yorkshireman, and when I answered to his descrip-

They all were glad the prodigal to see,
And some of them rejoiced over me.

In sin and folly I much time have spent,
These twenty years, since first to sea I went;
Sometimes I in the paths of virtue trod,
But found I loved pleasure more than God;
And while my mind was thus on pleasure bent,
The sabbath day was often idly spent;
Plays and romances did my senses please,
And then I thought there was no harm in these.
Sailors, beware of this enchanted ground,
'Twas there my deep depravity I found;
The foe within found out my weaker part,

tion, he said to the keeper of the chapel and others, more than once, that he was my own brother. The keeper of the chapel thought he saw the same person walking near the dock where the Dublin traders lay; he had said that he belonged to a vessel. I spent one afternoon walking round the docks, looking for this father; however, I looked for him in vain; at the same time hoping, if a brother he would find me out, and call on me. (Do you know any thing of the stranger alluded to, or were you then in Liverpool?) I waited a fortnight, but hearing nothing more of this brother, I wrote home to let the family know of this circumstance, part of an answer to which, from sister Martha, I will here transcribe; it is dated Kilham, Nov. 15th. She begins thus:

'Dear Brother,

'We received yours of the 9th instant, quite fortunate to come just the day before the fair, when brother David, uncle John, &c. were here; it is a very particular circumstance to me, the stranger calling at the chapel, and I hope will, in time, lead to a discovery, or some information concerning our dear and long lost brother Edward. Mother flatters herself much it is him. David says it is all nothing, there are so many Andersons. Uncle John says it must be him, for there is not a Henry Anderson in the list of Methodist preachers but yourself, besides his being a sailor too, is a sign of its being one of our family: it can be none else, except Christopher, and he sailed from London to the South Sea fishery last May. We had a letter from him dated Cape de Verd Islands, 2nd July, and it always is a ten or twelve months voyage, therefore, I hope and trust that Edward it must be.

'We have no real cause to suppose he is dead, and mother always did, and still thinks he will return. Whatever information you can get concerning him, be sure to send it us; and should it be him, O, how happy shall we all be at his return.'

Thus for Martha, and I think I have given it verbatim; you see what reasonings my letter has occasioned amongst the family at home. I shall send your letter inclosed this evening, so you may expect to hear from Kilham in a few days; O, how poor mother will rejoice to hear that you are still alive.

'I remain your loving brother,

'HENRY ANDERSON.'

To Mr. Edward Anderson, Mate of the Irene, Capt. Norris, Dublin.

Reason gave way, and pleasure won my heart;
Most other worldly pleasures I had prov'd,
Against them stood superior and unmov'd,
'Mongst women nature fail'd, and shew'd my heart,
Against their charms, this was my weakest part.
Shall I dissemble?    No, these lines sincere,
Paint but too glaring, and explain too clear.
Young Mistress Wanton met me on the way,
And she had many flattering things to say ;
With shame I own I felt my carnal mind
More than a little to her charms inclin'd.
These strong temptations suited to the flesh,
They came, and came, and came again afresh.
In vain amusements, feasting, dress, and play,
I often pass'd my precious time away ;
Of worldly happiness did idly dream,
Floating along, was driven with the stream;
Till God o'er me his chastening rod did shake,
Then I began out of my sleep to wake ;
His goodness would not let the captive go,
His love forbade my happiness below ;
My humble muse glows with a sacred flame,
While I exalt my great Redeemer's name;
Altho' proud sinners mock at what I say,
Yet will I still the love of God display ;
The world's contempt but makes its value rise
In my esteem, who all things else despise ;
The blood of Christ a strong dissolvent is,
'Tis this the heart can melt, and only this ;
His word, his love, and his kind look divine,
Can break the hardest heart, for it broke mine.
Preserv'd from dangers on the land and main,
I live to see my native home again ;

My friends had long suppos'd me dead or drown'd,
But now the dead's alive, the lost is found.
In vain amusements now no charms I see,
Since I found Christ, he's all in all to me.
For what are all the joys this world can give,
When fit to die we're only fit to live.
Now I the works of God can better scan,
And better taste the good design'd for man:
When we enjoy that love that casts out fear,
'Tis only then we can be happy here.
When first with Methodists at class I stood,
I thought how can they do me any good?
The leader I despised in my mind,
He was a basket maker, poor and blind.
'Twas by the teaching of this simple man, *
I saw the beauty of the gospel plan.
Some of the others like apostles spoke,
How they were sav'd from sin and satan's yoke,
And led by providence in various ways,
As marvellous as in our Saviour's days;
'Tis by experience only that we prove
How much these means contribute unto love;
And those who use them do with wonder find,
Them well adapted to improve the mind;
True Methodists a holy people are,
Who wage with sin and hell a constant war:
Call'd forth of God they make an open stand,

---

* The following passage is taken from the Homilies of the Church of England on Whitsuntide.—A certain philosopher, who being an enemy to Christ and his doctrine, could not be converted to the faith; but was able to withstand all the arguments that could be brought against him; at length there started up a poor simple man, one that was reported an ideot; the bishops and learned men standing by, were abashed, thinking they should all be put to open shame. But he brought the philosopher to such a point in the end, contrary to all expectations, that he could not but acknowledge the power of God in his word, and gave place to the truth. Was not this a marvellous work, that a silly soul of no learning should do that which many bishops of great learning and understanding were never able to bring about.

Against the open vices of the land ;
And those who fear'd they would make men go mad,
Now blush to think what little wit they had :
O may they to their calling boldly stand,
And cry aloud throughout this guilty land,
That sin is bringing on a dreadful storm,
Without a thorough and complete reform.

There is no instance in sacred or profane history of a rich, luxurious, immoral state ever reforming itself; it proceeds from bad to worse, till, in the course of God's providence, its fall is accomplished by the sword, by famine, or by pestilence. Notwithstanding this, the fall of every state may certainly be retarded by whatever retards the progress of vice.

*Bishop of Landaff's Sermon.*

"If the conjectures of Faber, and many other modern writers on the scripture prophecies, be well founded, then there are many who are now living will behold such calamities and judgments, as were never witnessed by any human being, since there was a nation upon earth. The strong intimations which God has afforded, through the appearances of the world, of the calamities that are impending, and of the prospect of brighter days which shall then succeed, conspire to tell mankind, that the day in which God shall judge the world in righteousness, is already on the wing. If those things are insufficient to alarm the guilty, neither will they be persuaded if one rose from the dead.

*Dr. Coke's Appendix to his Commentaries.*

According to Faber's explanation, the sixth vial ended in 1792, forty three years and six months for each vial. Rome will have drank her cup of indignation in 1817. The islands which were confederated with her will have fled away in 1822. The mountains or kingdoms of the west will not be found supporting the beast in the month of March, 1830. By the month of June, 1836, the great hail, or great invasion shall have fallen on the parties confederated with the Pope and Mahomet, and have swept away all their power. The destruction of the nations predicted by Zachariah, and the overthrow of the infidel kings, predicted by Daniel, will be cotemporary with the restoration of the Jews.

While, in these eventful days, we behold, on the one hand, the operation of error and of envy, labouring to suppress the efforts of truth and holy zeal: we see, on the other, the imbecility of all their projects. ' Great is the truth, and it will prevail,' it has already prevailed, and the laudable endeavours of Missionary Societies, Bible Societies, Tract Societies, and many other useful institutions, are evidently crowned with divine approbation and success. Thanks be to God, though a spirit of infidelity has spread through the old rotten churches in Europe, yet the gospel is spreading far and wide ; pious christians of all denominations are uniting together, to instruct the ignorant, and a holy zeal is kindled in the hearts of thousands, that will never be extinguished till all the ends of the earth have seen the salvation of God.

### END OF THE FIRST PART.

# PART SECOND.

Spring up, my muse, once more in humble style,
And on me may poetic genius smile,
And follow me as o'er the hills I roam,
To view the country round my native home,
And while enchanting prospects round I see,
Lord, give me grace to lift my heart to thee.
  One morn, at three o'clock, or little more,
I went from Flambro' Dikes to the North shore,
The weather fine, 'twas in the month of May,
Viewing those scenes I spent a pleasant day.
And there I saw the fish-market begun,
Numbers of fishing-boats on shore had run :
Large fish they threw in scores upon the beach,
Spread on the sand, and where the waves can't reach.
One values it, if that he cannot get,
He lowers it, the buyer cries out, 'Hett,'
As it is quick dispatch which they all wish,
Another in the boat sells the small fish.

To get soon done, who would not think it right,
That had been out, both wet and cold all night.
They but just speak, they pay no money down,
I never saw business dispatch'd so soon ;
The boats haul'd up, the waves may rage and foam,
Their work is done, the fishermen go home,
Some of them are content as heart could wish,
They rest all day, and all the night they fish.
I saw the fish pack'd up both great and small,
Then went to see a cave call'd the Life Hole ;*
There at the entrance struck with awe and dread,
I saw the ragged rocks hang o'er my head ;
Trembling I went, then all was dark before,
I heard within the foaming billows roar,
The winding passage still was dark as night,
But suddenly within appear'd a light.
When from the grave we into glory rise,
Then we must feel agreeable surprize ;
There I felt something similar to this,
Just like the prospect of eternal bliss ;
The light burst in, and soon dispers'd a l dread,
A vaulted arch appeared o'er my head,
Then I saw thro', as by an open door,
Under my feet seem'd a white marble floor,
I felt as into paradise restor'd,
I dropp'd upon my knees to praise the Lord.

* The Life Hole, or Robin Light Hole, has two openings, one communica-
ting with the land, the other the sea. The former is low and narrow, giving
solemn admission into the cavern ; which at the first entrance, is surrounded
with a tenebrious gloom ; but the darkness suddenly dispersing, the magnifi-
cence becomes unfolded, and excites the admiration of the exploring stranger.
The floor is a solid rock, white and bright as marble, formed into broad steps
of an easy descent ; and the stones at the sides are curiously variegated, and
appear something like china. The roof is finely arched, and near fifty feet high
at the centre ; the many projecting ledges, and fragments of suspended rocks,
joined to the great elevation, give it an awful, and at the same time, a majestic
appearance. On approaching the eastern extremity, a noble vista is formed by
its opening to the sea, which appears in the highest grandeur on emerging
from the gloom of the cavern.

The vaulted arch re-echoed the sound;
This place a pa'ace was, tho' under ground;
It shews the awful majesty of God,
Who but just spoke, and form'd it by a word.
On the cliff top I went when I came out,
There how delighted when I look'd about.
What a romantic scene beneath it lies,
I saw thousands of birds, and heard their cries.*
How far I've sail'd, what countries travell'd o'er,
Since I did stand upon this cliff before!
At Buckton I my father's flock did keep,
And I came here after some wild jock sheep,
Bred on the moors, no walls nor hedges hold,
Not us'd to be confin'd in fields or fold:
I durst not follow them so near the cliff,
So I went back and left them there adrift.
Not so my Saviour; where should I now be,
If the good Shepherd had not follow'd me?
I look'd with wondering eyes on every side,

* *Description of Flambro' Head.*—The cliffs at Flambro' are of amazing grandeur and tremendous height, from 150 to 200 yards perpendicular: they are composed of a mouldering limestone rock of a snowy whiteness, covered and adorned with a variety of birds, remarkable for the brilliancy of their plumage; from the latter end of April to the beginning of August myriads resort thither to build their nests, and trust their eggs and tender offspring to the exposed and dangerous security of broken rocks and projecting ledges. It is a high gratification to those who delight in the wild, the grand and the sublime, to view from the sea in calm weather this immense region of birds, and the diversified scenes of this stupendous promontory: at the report of a gun, the feathered inhabitants are instantly in motion; the eye is almost dazzled with the waving of innumerable wings, brightened by the rays of the sun, and the ear stunned with the clamour of their discordant notes; the strange dissonance of tone, resounding in the air from such a vast collection, accompanied by the solemn roar of the waves, dashing against rocks, and reverberated by the hollow caverns, (formed either by the restless turbulence of the ocean, gradually and imperceptibly excavating the solid rock, or by some unknown source of distant origin,) form a concert altogether rude and extraordinary, which effects the mind with unusual sensations.——There are al o many huge masses of white insulated rocks, of a pyramidial form, disjoined from the cliffs, either by the action of the sea, or some violent concussion, which raise their broken and irregular heads to a considerable elevation; these make a grotesque appearance and have stood the shock of many tempestuous winds.

(*Hinderwell's History of Scarbro.*)

D

As on a narrow ridge I sat astride;
Full sixty fathoms high above the main,
This scene it once would quite have turn'd my brain;
While sitting there, the rocks, the sea, the birds
Much contemplation to my mind affords;
Those high and rocky cliffs they shelter give,
And birds breed there that on the ocean live:
Tho' from the water they rise up so high,
Yet when they get on land they cannot fly;
Like flying fish, which I have often met,
They can't fly up but while their wings are wet,
By this unto their element confin'd,
Like all things else, answer the end design'd;
Here parrots, scoots, gulls, petrals make their
             haunts,
Hawks, pies, and pidgeons, crows and cormorants,
The rocks below o'er which the tide does flow,
There bait for fish, wilks, flithers, covens grow;
We see the providential plan display'd,
'Tis for the good of man that all are made;
There the smooth sea a pleasing sight affords,
Spread o'er with boats and ships, and swarms of birds.
   How many of my shipmates now are dead,
Since the first time I sail'd past Flambro' Head:
When I consider what I have deserv'd,
'Tis mercy all, that I have been preserv'd;
Just like a pinnacle that here I see,
It stands alone surrounded by the sea:
The rolling waves a constant war do wage,
But yet it still defies their utmost rage,
Tho' swelling high against its foot they beat,
And dash with violence—then again retreat;
They break themselves, but it abides their shock,

And when their rage is spent, there stands the rock;
It stands to shew the power of God design'd,
While waves the solid cliff has undermin'd.
Who trust in God, and on him constant call,
They safely stand when many strong ones fall
On sea, or land, or whereso'er they are,
Still are the *righteous God's peculiar care ;*
And from their heads one hair can never fall,
Unless permitted by the Lord of all.
My mind was still in meditation lost,
As I went on to view the signal post :
Likewise the curious signals that they use,
And a high tow'r which once was a light-house ;
From Burg, a fort, and from this light a flame,
This ancient town at first did take its name ;
Built by the Danes, their strongest fort was here,
Which by the dikes and castle does appear :
From hence intrenchments o'er the hills we trace,
This light * was kept that ships might find the place.
By this high tower to know it in the day,
The place they landed was Burlington Bay ;
And there whole fleets could safe at anchor ride,
Shelter'd by sands and cliffs from wind and tide.
And here the Danish dialect prevails,
More than elsewhere in England, Scotland, Wales,

* A new Light-House is erected about four hundred yards within the extreme point of the Head, close to a Bluff on the south side of Silex Bay, which is the only place near the Head where a boat can land, and people ascend the cliff.

The light is a revolving light, with three faces, of seven reflectors each ; and in order to distinguish it from the revolving lights of Tinmouth and Cromer: which shews a face every minute, this light on Flambro' Head will exhibit a face every two minutes, and one of them coloured red, whereby the light from that face being diminished, it will not, in hazy weather, or at a great distance be visible so far, or so strong, as the other two faces: and when, in such cases, only two faces are seen, the interval of time between them will be two minutes and four minutes alternately, which will sufficiently distinguish this light from any other light in the kingdom.

" Git the gene heame, stcck'd haver leher deer,"
These in their common language still appear.
Oft in the night I careful hove the lead,
As we our course did steer past Flambro' Head;
Thick weather, when afraid to come too nigh,
Then we observ'd which way the birds did fly.
When at a distance, and no land in sight,
The birds our pilots, they direct us right.
As I sail'd past one fine and pleasant day,
When I had been for many years away;
And as I walk'd the deck, and plow'd the deep,
Viewing the hills where I oft tended sheep;
Ready to cry, as by them swift we past,
" Why was my lot upon the ocean cast?"
A prospect of the castle, town and mill,*
I had from off the top of Beacon Hill;
Its ancient strength it there my fancy strikes,
The cliffs so high, and fortified by dikes;
All round the Head I view'd the ocean wide,
Burlington Bay, where ships at anchor ride;
Likewise the shipping, lying in Key pier,
The country round delightful did appear.
When to the westward there I turn my eyes,
And on the hills see large plantations rise;
In Holderness, where stagnant water stood,
Now drains are cut, they seek their native flood;
There shaking bogs were dangerous to pass,
Where nought but rushes grew, and sedgy grass;
For rotting sheep those places were well known,
They now are dry, and cloth'd with smiling corn;

* Mills anciently belonged to Lords of manors: tenants were only permitted to grind at the lord's mill; nor could they erect a mill without a special indulgence of the lord.

May they go on to dry each bog and car,
And leave no stagnant pool but Hornsey Mar :*
Many go there to fish for pleasure's sake,
But they must always pay for what they take ;
When caught, they weigh it at the New Inn door,
The money it is given to the poor.
This lake is two miles long, and one mile broad,
And both with fish and fowl it is well stor'd ;
And in the midst of it an island lies,
Where sea birds breed, for miles you hear their cries.
I went there in a boat, one morn in spring,
The cries around me made my ears to ring ;
Thousands of birds were flying round my head,
So many nests, that clear I could not tread,
Without breaking their eggs, in vain to strive,
And with young birds, the weeds seem'd all alive ;
The old ones cry'd ; "Begone," they seem'd to say,
And flew close at me as I went away ;
The swans so stately held their heads so high,
They too did hiss me as I pass'd them by ;
They flapp'd their wings, and at me they did stare,

Odo, the first earl of Holderness, came over with William the Conqueror : who, at the intercession of the archbishop of Roan, gave him the seniority of Holderness, on condition, that in every expedition in which the archbishop attended in person, Odo should be the standard-bearer, with twelve knights.

When Odo came to settle in Holderness in 1066, he found it a barren country, bearing nothing but oats ; he therefore requested of the king some lands that would bear wheat: the king consented and granted him the lordship of Bytham in Lincolnshire. The grant was made to Stephen, son of Odo, to feed his son William, then an infant, with wheaten bread ; who afterwards became a great warrior, and was commonly called William Le Gross. *(the Fat.)*

It appears from an ancient record, that in the year 1346, John Monceaux was Lord of the manor of Barmston, in Holderness. The profession of arms being then esteemed the most honourable employment, he consigned the cultivation of his lands chiefly to his customary tenants. The yearly rent of the whole Lordship was 37l. 12s. hens at Christmas 17 ; offering, silver paid, at Christmas 119 shillings ; eggs at Easter 1695 ; pepper two pound : cumming seed two pound ; plowing or harrowing days were thirty two and a half ; reaping days thirty three ; leading days in harvest with a wain or cart, fifty.

Tradition says, Hornsey Church was built ten miles from the sea, which is now come within one mile. In Doomsday book are recorded a number of Hamlets, Towns, and Villages ; which have been washed away by the devastations of the sea and the River Humber, whose very names are totally forgot.
*Dade's History of Holderness.*

And seem' to say, "What bus'ness have you there?"
I never saw in countries I've gone o'er,
So many in so small a spot before.
As I look'd round my wond'ring eye beholds,
The vast improvements on the Yorkshire Wolds;*
When on the top of Weatrop-hill I stand,
A prospect opens over sea and land;
Charm'd with the view that there around me lies,
Both sea and hills, they seem'd to touch the skies:
As o'er this vale I take a wide survey,
And view the hills where I oft us'd to play;
Drove out from thence, my father's farm was sold;
We Lutton left when I was nine years old:
This seem'd a cross not rightly understood,
But afterwards we saw it work for good.
Tho' it was but eight miles we then remov'd,
To Kilham; a far better place it prov'd;
There all inclos'd, the diff'rence shew'd as plain,
As from the wilderness into Canaan:
There I got finer clothes and better meat,
We eat no barley there, but liv'd on wheat.

To see my friends, to Lutton oft I went,
Together many pleasant hours we spent;
My aunt and uncle Lovel liv'd there still:
At Helperthorp my uncles Dick and Will;
At Weaverthorp relations did not fail,
For there my uncles George and Tom sold ale:
My uncle John there keeps a blacksmith's shop,

*The Wolds are the most magnificent assemblages of chalky hills this island affords; and their culture has been much improved, and many of the hills are decorated with plantations. The late Sir. Christopher Sykes had the honour of being the most extensive planter. The pages of history have blazoned the deed sof heroes: who in the career of ambition and conquest, have subdued and desolated fruitful provinces; but how much more dignified a character in the eye of reason, is he who cloathes the land with the beauties of a new creation, and converts a barren waste into a fertile region? King William, the Conqueror, laid this country waste from the Humber to the River Tees.

And at my grandmother's I us'd to stop ;
And our relations there did all resort,
At Candlemas they met at Weatrop sport.
My uncles I could reckon up eighteen,
And fifty cousins, where I've welcome been
How pleas'd was I so many friends to see,
This always was a feast indeed to me :
Distant relations, far as we could ken,
Both rich and poor, they all were welcome then ;
And freely all on uncle John did call,
If he had room he entertain'd them all,
I always saw this town with joy,
For there I went to school when but a boy ;
Then no ambitious views my mind did fill,
Those times I think upon with pleasure still,
In the Dale towns their management at best,
It seem'd a hundred years behind the rest ;
Some little farms were spread o'er many a mile,
To see their management would make you smile :
Half of their lands lay waste, so poor laid down
They could not get manure so far from town.
I've seen them plowing with a cow and ass,
And harrows driven by a servant lass ;
Manure on little heaps they us'd to lay,
Near to the town, few got it far away ;
Out of the wet farm-yards they did it draw,
It lay and dry'd till it was just like straw ;
And when spread out, it was so full of seeds,
Instead of corn, it only grew more weeds.
In fallow fields, a crop of thistles grew,
Their downy seeds about the country flew ;
In vain, from scab their flocks they try to keep,
They oft were smitten by their neighbour's sheep ;

How chang'd since the last time I went that way,
No hedges then, their fields all open lay :
Now roads are chang'd, houses built in the field,
All new inclos'd as far as Whimmore Bield ;
Old Swarth is now turn'd into tillage land,
And a new course of husbandry is plann'd ;
Their common method is to pare and burn,
And there the ling and whins a,e almost gone.
On Shirburn brow, I view the country o'er,
And a vast prospect opens out before :
Looking due north, I see the high Moor Hills,
And the Low Lands the fruitful valley fills,
Where turf was cut they now have cut a drain,*
The flowing Car is now a fertile plain ;
On barren hills scarce ought but flints and stones,
A few short whins, and strew'd with dead sheep's bones
On those cold hills now large plantations rise,
And blooming cinque-foil there delight your eyes.
In summer, for a charming country seat,
Wold cottage is allow'd the most complete ;
Own'd by a man of literary fame,
And captain Topham is his comman name.
There art and nature both unite their smiles ;
This from my mother's house is not five miles.
A monument stands there for all to view :
Of the most curious thing I ever knew :
A stone is kept which fell down from above,
And serves the wond'rous pow'r of God to prove :
In ninety-five it fell down on the ground,

*The Act of Parliament for the Drainage, was obtained in 1800.
The actual improvement of this is almost incalculable ; from a state of nearly
resembling Ovid's Poetical Chaos : it has been universally brought under the
plough, and in some instances produces not less than 12 quarters per acre.—
History of Scarbro'.

Lenth thirty inches, weight fifty-six pound ; *
It sunk into the ground and pierc'd a rock,
The people in Woldnewton felt the shock :
Two persons saw it when it struck the ground,
And the report was heard for ten miles round :
'Twas seen to smoak—was hot when first it fell.
But where it came from, no one yet can tell :
Wond'rous the cause, and fruitless to enquire,
Our wisest part is humbly to admire :
Beyond all human reason to explore,
It ought to make us fear the Lord the more,
What else is worth our care but him to please,
Who can command such miracles as these,
Since I came home, as I this country view,
The towns, the fields, now ev'ry thing looks new ;
The old thatch'd cottages have ta'en their flight,
And new til'd houses now appear in sight ;

*The following is extracted from Major Topham's account of the stone.*

* " It was on Sunday about five o'clock, the thirteenth of December in the year 1795, that the stone in question fell two fields from my house. The weather was misty, and at times, inclining to rain ; and though there were some thunder and light'ning at a distance, it was not till the falling of the stone that the explosion took place which alarmed the surrounding country, and which created so distinctly the sensation, that something very singular had happened.

When the stone fell, a shepherd of mine, who was returning from the sheep, was about one hundred and fifty yards from the spot ; George Sawden, a carpenter, was passing within sixty yards ; and John Shipley one of my farming servants, was so near the spot where it fell, that he was struck very forcibly by some of the mud and earth raised by the stone dashing into the earth, which it penetrated to the depth of twelve inches, and seven afterwards into the chalk rock, making in all a depth of nineteen inches from the surface.

While the stone was passing through the air, which it did in a North East direction from the sea-coast, numbers of persons distinguished a body moving through the clouds though not able to ascertain what it was : and two sons of the clergyman of Wold-Newton (a village near me) saw it pass so distinctly by them, that they ran immediately to my house, to know if any thing extraordinary had happened.

" The stone in its fall excavated a place of the depth before mentioned, and of something more than a yard in diameter. It had fixed itself so strongly in the chalk rock, that it required some labour to dig it out."

The breadth of the stone was twenty eight inches, the length thirty inches, and the weight fifty-six pounds.

To distinguish the spot where the stone fell, Major Topham has erected a pillar (with an appropriate inscription) surrounded by a plantation. The stone is preserved in Mr. Sowerby's collection, Lambeth.

*(History of Scarbro'.)*

But when the town of Kilham first I saw, ‡

The walls were mostly clay, and thatch'd with straw,

What alterations in a little while!

The houses now are mostly brick and tile:

They've built a poor-house, and a large new mill,

And cut away How, Butt, and Butcher Hill;

Besides improvements which the town does yield,

We see new houses built about the field;

A diff'rent view we see at the town end,

Where boys they us'd the geese and pigs to tend:

You saw the green spread o'er with geese and feathers,

And cattle then confin'd with stakes and tethers:

The corn destroy'd, all round the town you saw,

And for some distance, nothing left but straw.

Since 'twas inclos'd but nine and thirty years,

The ground is much improv'd, it now appears;

‡ Kilham is an ancient market town, situated in a pleasant valley, at the South-east declivity of the Wolds, adjoining the flat country called Holderness.

The open fields, containing 7000 acres, were inclosed in the year 1772, and great improvements have been made in the cultivation, the plantations affording shelter both for corn and cattle. It appears to have been far more populous than it is at present by the ancient scites of houses and vestages of buildings. There is a remarkable spring which sometimes breaks out after a wet Autumn at a place called Henpit-Nole, on the road to Langtoft, after it has been dry 15 or 20 years, and has frequently done considerable damage. There is a round hill near the road to Pocthorp, called Gallows Hill, where sculls and human bones are yet to be found. Kilham may have been the residence of some chief or warrior, who reigned absolute and hanged who he pleased, as was the case amongst the Danes and Saxons.

There is a piece of ground called Danes Graves in the South west extremity of the lordship, marked with a number of little hillocks close to one another, supposed to be the burial place of the Danes after a great battle. It was the custom for their companions in arms, to carry each a helmet of earth to strew over the grave as a last tribute of affection.

The Danes had a fortified camp at Flambro', and the king of Northumberland had a royal residence at Driffield, four miles from this spot, and one of their kings by the name of Alfred was buried there, as appears from the following inscription to his memory: within the chancel of the church at little Driffield: —" Here lies the body of Alfred, king of Northumberland, who departed this life Jan. 19th 705, in the 20th year of his reign."—At Ebeston there is a small cave, called Alfred's Cave: In this, as tradition reports, a Saxon king of that name flying wounded from his pursuers, took shelter, and remained there one night, was the next day carried to Driffield, where he died.

The following inscription engraved, on stone, over the cave and afterwards painted on wood, when the stone decayed, is still remembered by some of the ancient inhabitants;—" Alfred, king of Northumberland, was wounded in a bloody battle near this place, and was removed to little Driffield, where he lies buried, hard by his intrenchments may be seen."—An inclosure at the West end of Ebeston, adjoining the Pickering-road, still goes by the name of Bloody Close which strongly indicates that a battle has been fought there.

The springing corn which oft has blasted been,
By frosty winds, so cold, so sharp and keen,
Now shelter'd is, no more the storm need dread,
But cheerful lifts its little drooping head ;
The cattle they no shelter then could find,
Except in dales where sun scarce ever shin'd :
Screen'd by the trees, now in the shade can lay,
On hills find shelter in a stormy day ;
The sheep that oft were lost in drifts of snow,
Shepherds to find them knew not where to go ;
When drifted now, can easily be found,
The fences keep them on their owners ground,
In harvest when it came a windy day,
The sheaves and peas-reaps oft were blown away,
Mixt, and against some balk or hill were blown,
The farmers then they could not know their own ;
Some then would take advantage of the rest,
At such a time the strongest man far'd best;
This caus'd disputes which they could not prevent,
Some suff'ring loss were forc'd to be content ;
Neighbour 'gainst neighbour had perpetual jars,
Town against town were constantly at wars ;
He who so rash as for his friend durst plead,
Was like to get a blow or broken head ;
They seldom then did to the lawyer go,
Disputes were mostly settled by club-law :
What reason have we know for thanks and praise,
That we were bred and born in gospel days ;
Then after church upon the sabbath-day,
Both old and young would run to foot-ball play;
The only prize they could expect to win,
Was to get broken leg, or broken shin.
But as to morals, now, by saving grace,

The people are improv'd as well as place;
Some centuries back, how ignorant and rude,
In what a wretched state of servitude;*
On Sundays now, instead of foot-ball play,
You see them meet together now to pray;
Some for amusement, that despise their name,
Yet come to hear, disturb them, and make game;
Tho' they have gone to school without dispute,
They're unrefin'd, scarce rais'd above the brutes
Altho' the gospel light so clear has shin'd,
Yet many still are ignorant and blind;
While some that are without school-education,
Have put on Christ are wise unto salvation.
Our knowledge all will prove a wild goose chase,
Except we come into the school of grace,
    "While I delightful country scenes admire,
    "They tune my numbers and my muse inspire;
    "A twofold joy fills my enraptur'd mind,
    "With gratitude and admiration join'd.

---

*At Rudstone, a village near Kilham, in the church yard, is a large stone 29 feet high above the ground, and it has been traced to the depth of twelve below, without reaching the foundation. It is supposed to have been placed there by our ancestors when they worshipped stocks and stones.

In the year 1329, J. Ward, rector of Barmston, conveyed to Wm. Monceaux and Margaret his wife, under certain limitations, some lands in that lordship, together with the bodies of John and Robert Kidwit, their villaines or bondmen by birth, and their whole issue and effects.

In the reign of Richard the second, Richard De Swathorp, Knight, in consideration of one mark of silver (13s. 4d.) released to Wm. De. Boynton, his right in the person of Berchard De Swathorp and his whole family and stock. The above grant is still in the possession of Sir Francis Boynton.

In the year 1514 king Henry the 8th, manumitted two of his villaines in the following form:

"Whereas God created all men free, but afterwards the laws and customs of nations subjected some under the yoke of servitude, we think it pious and meritorious with God to manumit Henry Knight a Taylor, and John Helm, a Husbandman our natives, as being born within our manor of Chymisland, in our county of Cornwell, together with all their issue, born or to be born, and all their goods, lands and chattels, so as the said persons and their issue shall, from henceforth be of free condition by us &c."

This form of infrancisement explains the general condition of the people, if born within a certain district, they and their issue were the bondmen of the lord of the manor and all their property, besides this, they could not leave the manor on which they were from their birth in a state of servitude, without the leave of their lord.—*Dades History of Holderness.*

"Tho' fortune does her golden gifts deny,
"She cannot shut the windows of the sky;
"She cannot rob me of free nature's grace,
"I scorn her frowns, while I these beauties trace,
"'Tis done,' I cry'd, 'the great deciding part,
"The world's subdu'd, and God has all my heart;
"Celestial passions kindle in my soul,
"And ev'ry mean inglorious thought controul."
O, may my tongue, my heart, and life make known,
The mercies which the Lord to me has shown:
Sav'd me from the brink of hell, the sea, the grave,
I stand a witness of his pow'r to save.
If I don't praise the Lord with heart sincere,
All nature cries aloud against me here.
"In all my wanderings round this world of care,
"In all my griefs and God has giv'n-a share;
"I still had hopes, for pride attends us still,
"Amidst the swains, to shew my book learn'd skill;
"I still had hopes—my long vexations past,
"Here to return and die at home at last.
O, what reflections do my thoughts supply,
In the church yard were both my parents lie;
Viewing their graves, fresh in my mind recall,
My mother's death, a brother's early fall,
Altho' this theme may not give much delight,
A subject great, engages me to write:
A loving mother taken from our view,
And to her mem'ry these few lines are due:
In midst of troubles, sickuess, and much pain,
She testify'd that she was born again;
And patient waited, willing to depart,
'Twas plain to see that grace had chang'd her heart;
To save the lost, she knew the Saviour came,

E

And with her latest breath she lisp'd his name;
While seven of her children, round her bed,
Were on their knees, her happy spirit fled;
She seem'd to smile on death and troubles past,
Then calmly fell asleep, and slept her last.
One of her sons, tho' in another clime—
He thought he saw her at that very time;
He offer'd her a kiss—she never spoke,
But smil'd on him—then vanish'd—he awoke:
Tho' much astonish'd yet he felt no dread,
But from that time he fancy'd she was dead;
He told his ship-mates, but they laugh'd at him,
And said, 'twas but a dream, an idle whim;
But when a letter came, and it prov'd true
His ship-mates then were much astonish'd too:
We see what love for children mothers have,
In her, it seem'd to reach beyond the grave:
Five sons she had at sea, for many years,
And often they have cost her floods of tears;
She who could scarcely bear them out of sight,
What must she feel when they forgot to write!
O that each careless prodigal like me,
May now his duty to his parents see:
Duty compels me for such love and pains,
To pay a tribute to her last remains;
While seven children follow her along,
They join together in a mournful song;
They mixt their tears, with sorrow sympathize—
There not a stranger, but a mother lies!
Some will remember to their dying day,
With what reluctancy they went away,
From yonder spot, where now her body lies,
With solemn steps, and with heart rending cries;

We cannot soon forget this solemn hour,
But time these strong impressions does devour.
May this occasion speak to ev'ry heart,
Prepare yourselves, you likewise must depart;
Depart for ever from this mortal life,
Your dearest friendships, children, father, wife.
Let all attend this lesson to improve,
And learn their state before they hence remove;
And wisdom gain from sickness, death the grave,
And fly to Jesu's blood, their souls to save:
They who believe in him, altho' they die,
For ever reign enthron'd above the sky.

For sev'nty-three revolving tedious years,
My father sojourn'd in this vale of tears;
His toil and care to farming was apply'd,
In which simplicity he liv'd and dy'd:
His ancestors were farmers round this place
Two hundred years ago their names we trace;
May we amongst the poor be kind and free,
And imitate his hospitality:
"Some vainly boast of pedigree and blood,
" He's, truly noble, that is just and good;
" How blest is he who crowns in shades like these,
" A youth of labour with an age of ease;
" Yes, let the rich deride, the proud disdain,
" These simple blessings of the lowly train:

* In examining the parish register, I find my great grandfather, Henry Anderson, was born at Cottam in 1621; he had been a soldier, and away from home many years. It is said that when he came back he was so altered, that his mother could not believe that he was her son, until he shewed her a mole, or mark, which she remembered when he was a child. My grandfather Thomas Anderson, was born at Cottam in 1664, but removed to East Lutton; he married at thirty-five years of age; his first wife had eight sons and one daughter; he married again at sixty-one years of age; his second wife had five sons and one daughter, who were all living when he died in 1744, aged eighty-three years and by his desire was carried to his grave by eight of his own sons. My father, Robert Anderson, was the oldest son by the second wife; at thirty-seven years of age he married Elizabeth Robson, who was then but seventeen: when she was christened, her mother said to him, "Who knows but this child may become your wife; and this prediction came to pass.

" To me more dear congenial to my heart,
" One native charm, than all the gloss of art ;
Listen ye proud, be this to misers told,
That gen'rous souls can scorn their wretched gold ;
That doing good to them to pleasure yields,
Unknown to honour's slaves in bloody fields ;
They live content, amidst domestic joys,
And scorn the world with all its glitt'ing toys ;
He liv'd from noise of war and danger free,
And dy'd in peace amidst his family ;
Bless'd with a num'rous offspring, his delight ;
Of females two, of males the number eight ;
The eldest first abandon'd husbandry,
And went to try his fortune on the sea ;
For twenty years he plow'd the raging main,
Has often traded into France and Spain ;
And out of Hull he many voyages made,
Had the Britannia in the Hambro' trade.
The second was employ'd in tending sheep,
But at eighteen he went to plough the deep ;
And out of London many voyages made,
Had the Jemima in the Lisbon trade.
By friends advanc'd as providence decreed,
His worldly prospects once were fair indeed ;
All promis'd well, but promises are vain,
Those whom he dealt with, lov'd the paths of gain ;
Of his misfortunes they advantage made,
So he determin'd to leave off that trade,
And fly far distant from ambitious strife,
To steal along the vale of humble life :
In calm retirement, there to meditate,
Upon a future and eternal state,
The third left home but with a diff'rent view,

And other motives led him to pursue,
To seek the souls of men, by error led,
Points to that blood which for their sins was shed;
Tells them, like Wesley, Christ is all they want,
Now he's a preacher, an Itinerant.
The fourth left home, but till'd the ground the same,
He follow'd culture by another name;
In gardening employ'd, as the first man,
And Adam's works his genius did scan;
He join'd the methodists, took their advice,
And from his garden, looks to Paradise.
The fifth a farmer bred, he staid at home,
Had no cur'osity abroad to roam,
The sixth she has for Jesus all resign'd,
And to serve God her heart is yet inclin'd.
The seventh, when young at home he would not stay,
But went to sea, was press'd, and led away;
Thro' perils great, his country's cause to serve,
Owes all to God, who did his life prerve,
From raging seas, and dangers greater far,
When master of the Prince, at Trafalgar:
Rouse up my muse, describe with all thy might,
The glories and the terror of that fight;
The French and Spaniards, when the fight begun,
Were well prepar'd, did all that could be done;
But all this caution was of no avail,
Nelson had laid a plan it scarce could fail;
A British fleet to conquer, a proud Don,
But want an Admiral to lead them on:
"Come follow me my boys," was Nelsons cry,
Determin'd then to conquer or to die;
He valu'd honour more than life or limb,
To see them, was to conquer them with him;

He said, " My signals if you cannot see,
" Make no delay, example take by me:
" To know your foes thro' smoke, or in the dark,
" Engage them close, you cannot miss your mark:"
Then he led on, and through their line  he broke,
And put them to confusion by that stroke:
The English cannons then so well did play,
Some of them soon were glad to get away:
What dreadful havoc! O what scenes were there!
Some sinking, and some flying in the air:
More than the rest, this casts a damp on all,
When they first heard of gallant Nelson's fall!
We must submit to Him who rules on high,
The coward and the brave they all must die;
And he who weather'd out so many storms,
Alas! is now become a prey for worms.
This lesson shews us, if we but attend,
How soon all worldly grandeur's at an end.
These victories which we rejoice to hear,
Are dearly bought; cost many a widow's tear,*
Say not when you those mournful Lines explore,
The valiant Hero falls to rise no more.
When the last trump shall sound thro' earth and air,

Rev. VICESSIMUS KNOX, D. D.

* The causes of war are for the most part such as must disgrace an anima
pretending to rationality.  Two poor mortals, elevated with the distinction of
a golden bauble on their heads, called a crown, take offence at each other with-
out any reason, or with the very bad one of wishing for an opportunity of ag-
grandizing themselves, by making reciprocal depredations.  The *creatures of
the court* and the *leading men* of the *nation*, who are usually under the influence
of the court, resolve *(for it is their interest)* to *support* their royal master, and
are never at a loss to invent some colourable pretence for engaging the nation
in the horrors of war.  Taxes of the most burthensome kind are levied, sol-
diers are collected, so as to leave a scarcity of husbandmen, reviews, and en-
campments succeed, and at last, *fifteen or twenty thousand men meet on a plain,
and coolly shed each other's blood without the smallest personal animosity or the sha-
dow of a provocation.* The *kings* in the mean time, and the grandees, who have
employed these poor innocent *victims* to shoot bullets at each other's heads,
remain quietly at home, and *amuse themselves*, in the intervals of balls, hunting
schemes and pleasures of every species, *with reading at the fire-side, over a cup
of chocolate the dispatches from the army, and the news in the extraordinary gazette.*

Ye dead arise for Judgment now prepare.
Honour will be of no advantage then,
But heroes must be try'd like other men.
That which by men most highly is esteem'd,
With God is an abomination deem'd,
How happy then are they who learn to know,
The will of God and do it here below.
Calm and serene they take their cheerful way,
Through life short span, to everlasting day,
The eighth, she is to reading much inclin'd,
And by that means has much improv'd her mind :
Her mother's comfort was her chiefest care,
In her last illness, she was always there.
May natural affection bind us all,
For without that our piety is small.
Ninth, for a Lisbon merchant was design'd,
But on the land he could not be confin'd ;
It seems he brav'd all dangers without fear,
When captain of the Bull dog privateer.
Now he has left the privateering trade,
And master in the navy has been made ;
He guides a ship, now wicked who can tell ?
By some compared, to a floating hell;
We see that where temptations most abound,
The more extremely wicked men are found ;
But where temptation may not be so great,
By nature all are in a lost estate :
The ancient promise which old Adam view'd,
Was made to all the race, in Christ renew'd,
Those therefore are the objects of his love,
He dy'd, arose, and reigns for them above ;
His blood to plead, his blessings to impart,
And to reveal himself to ev'ry heart ;

Some of them fear the Lord, support his cause,
And shew they have respect to all his laws;
They often on the word of God attend,
And gladly hearken to the sinner's Friend,
And wonder at his condescending grace,
In acts of mercy to the human race.
The tenth, a farmer was design'd to be,
But since his father dy'd he went to sea:
His ardent bosom panted after fame;
He fondly hop'd to signalize his name;
Resolv'd in honour's field, to try his fate;
He enter'd in the navy, master's mate;
But ah! before his valour it was try'd,
He broke a blood-vessel, came home, and dy'd.

    These were his offsprings whom he dearly lov'd,
And a kind father to them all he prov'd;
He gave no cause for any to suspect,
That to another he shew'd more respect,
His care and tenderness for all was such,
The danger lay in loving them too much.
In all their minds the powers of reason shone,
And well proportion'd all their bodies grown:
Whenever he upon them cast an eye,
'Twas cause of gratitude to the Most High.
Now he is gone, and we are left behind,
To be a curse or blessing to mankind;
To fill up stations both by sea and land,
To be subordinate, or give command;
To rear up families which far may spread,
The name of Anderson when we are dead.
If justice, mercy, and a humble heart,
We must esteem, and chuse the better part;
Then to the world our faith will prove divine,

And many hearts we may to truth incline.
If with the greatest privileges blest,
We in a state of carelessness do rest,
Then God will make his judgments dreadful shine,
Resent his injur'd rights of love divine.

Our parents gone—who next by death may fall
A sacrifice, precarious is to all!
We therefore should each one this question try,
Upon our hearts, and say " Lord is it I ?
We all the debt of nature soon must pay,
We should begin while it is call'd to day ;
And if we wise unto salvation be,
From guilt and sin we all may be set free :
Death with his sting shall lose its pointed dart,
And glorious prospects gladden every heart:
Of faith possess'd in the Redeemer's blood,
Our bodies made a temple, meet for God ;
Our commerce with the world we then may drop,
And lay our bodies down in cheerful hope,
That one day he will raise them from the dead,
And make them like to Christ, our living Head ;
The subject of our happy theme shall be—
*Redeeming love*, to all eternity !

* Eternity !!! gracious God. how terrible to bad men, how pleasurable to good men, how interesting to all, is the thought of everlasting existence, it is a thought which if rooted firmly in the heart by faith, if cherished therein by repeated reflections, would of itself, reform the morals of mankind.
Everlasting existence !!! ambitious Tyrants of the earth : relentless Murderers of mankind ; think on this, extortioners oppressors of the poor, think on this, drunkards, swearers, sabbath breakers. ridiculers of the Religion of Christ, think on this, sensual confirmists to the foolish fashions of the world, think on this, O let not a propensity to vice blind your understandings, read the gospel, it will tell you the danger of passion; uncontroul'd, in it you will find the anchor of a christian's hope, the fact of the resurrection of Christ, fully established, and consequently the certainty of your own.

## END OF THE SECOND PART.

# PART THIRD.

MAY heav'nly wisdom still my muse inspire,
And fill my bosom with seraphic fire.
Well I remember still the great surprise,
When first the ocean met my wond'ring eyes;
Wide o'er the blue expanse my eager sight,
Beheld the distant bark, with sails of white,
But then it never enter'd in my brain,
That ever I should plow the raging main;
But there's a Providence that rules on high,
Who guards his children with a watchful eye;
And places them according to his will,
Just in the spot they are design'd to fill:
Whatever business he has call'd us to,
Amidst all dangers he can bring us thro'.
After a dark and dismal stormy night,
The morning dawns, the port appears in sight;
Our fears are fled, the pilot boat appears,
And all things round a pleasing aspect wears;
    Our friends they hear our ship is come in sight,
The signal's hoist, they view it with delight;
Rejoice that soon we shall each other see,

For they have oft been looking out for me.
What gratitude I felt to Heav'n above;
Once more I shall embrace the friends I love:
My pulse beat high, the town appear'd in view,
I felt a pleasure landsmen never knew.

    Help me to paint, let genius guide the tool,
While I a picture draw of Liverpool;
Prospective muse, attend my willing hands,
To shew the beauties that this view commands?—
Here rise the numerous buildings, great and small,
The 'Change and Churches overlook them all;
The smoke in columns rises in the wind,
Darkens the air, and leaves a veil behind;
Rising from forges, and from fact'ries new;
The wind-mills on the hills next strike your view;
When the wind blows, you see them night and morn,
Keep turning round to grind the people corn.
When on the shipping here we cast our eyes,
We see 'midst buildings, woods of masts arise;
Likewise the ships that in the river lie,
And boats across it, as they constant ply;
When on the ocean we begin to look,
The river then seems like a littlte brook:
We see the shipping coming in from far,
And others going out, prepar'd for war.
The wind comes fair, then brooking no delay,
They, at high water, soon got under way;
Each wishing to be first, they eager try,
And ev'ry sail unto the wind apply:
'Tis not enough that sailors risk their lives,
But they must leave their sweethearts and their wives,
The boatman calls, he's waiting along-side—
" Must we be parted," says a new made bride;
Torn from the joys the honey moon affords,

Her looks express her feelings more than words;
Her Husband says, " My absence do not mourn,
" These happy days again will soon return ;
And while he stops to take a last embrace,
The pilot calls him to attend his place,
They hand her down the side, all bath'd in tears,
She waves her hand, the sailors give three cheers ;
She sees them crow'd along the Cheshire shore ;
When round the rock she sees the ship no more !
She prays the Lord to keep him from all harms,
And bring him safe unto her longing arms.
Thro' the Rock Channel, safe the pilot steers,
Hard by the sands, which white with surf appears ;
And there the dang'rous banks stretch'd far and wide,
More dang'rous render'd by the rapid tide ;
The leadsman cheerly tells the depth along,
While the whole ship's responsive to his song ;
When past the buoys, and clear of ev'ry sand,
With a fine breeze they leave the less'ning land,
With rials set and stunsails on each side,
Fearless they stretch across the ocean wide.

 As on the sea my eyes are fixed still,
A flag is hoisted on the Bidston Hill ;*

*For the convenience and more readily informing the merchants what ships are approaching the town, the greatest part of them have signals on poles placed near the light-house on Bidston-hill, in Cheshire, which commands both Formby and Rock channels, the two principal entrances to the river. There are at this time fifty-eight, of which forty-nine belong to particular merchants, the remainder are to distinguish and shew if the vessels coming in are Greenlanders, men of war, or if the vessel is ship, brig, or snow; there are also immediate signals to the town of all vessels seen in distress in either of the channels, that thereby speedy assistance may be given. The method used to convey intelligence to the town, so as to inform every merchant of the arrival of his ship, is for the masters of the several vessels, as soon as they make the light-house, to hoist a particular signal, which is previously agreed, to to denote the respective merchant to whom the ship belongs; this being seen from the signal-house, instantly directs what flag to hoist for the information of the merchant on shore; these signals on a clear day may be seen from St. James's Walk, &c. by the naked eye, as far as the N. W. buoy, and in hazy weather easily distinguished by good glasses from thence, or from any of the lower parts of the town. This is a most eligible and commendable plan, and of greater utility than that of Maker Tower at Plymouth, which is partial in it signals, whereas this being general, is what no other part of the kingdom can boast.

A signal for a ship that's homeward bound—
She proves a prize worth twenty thousand pound ;
The bells they ring, the ship she comes in sight,
And crouds of people view her with delight.

    My brother sailors all who share this prize,
Spend not like fools, nor good advice despise ;
Nor idly squander round the tavern fires,
The money your own family requires ;
At home you may have a domestic feast,
But don't get drunk, and make yourself a beast ;
Behold the man addicted to this crime,
What loss sustain'd of health, wealth, peace and time ;
How far beneath the brute, how base his fall,
You would not think him rational at all.
Sailors no more disgrace the British name—
A drunken English seaman—what a shame !
Whose character's so much above the rest,
Yet he, when drunk, is ev'ry body's jest.
Now, by a brother sailor, be advis'd,
Rise from your fall, and be no more despis'd ;
You who have gain'd your country so much fame,
That all the world may still respect the name ;
For British seamen that have sober prov'd,
In foreign parts are much esteem'd and lov'd,
When just come home, and free from care and strife,
I see a sailor and his loving wife ;
To see a child sit smiling on his knee,
Was always a most pleasing sight to me ;
Delightful scene, when two congenial minds,
Whom nature pairs, and lawful marriage binds ;
When kind affection feeds the kindled flame,
And friendship yields but to a dearer name ;
Their fair example must at once inspire,

A wish to copy what all must admire.
Amongst my pious friends divinely taught,
A happy pair oft my attention caught:
Both with exulting hearts could sweetly tell,
How Jesus sav'd them from the lowest hell;
And gave them hearts to love his sacred ways,
And to delight in shewing forth his praise:
Ye single men I charge you on your lives,
Be very careful how you chuse your wives;
What is the beauty of the fairest face,
Without the charms of modesty and grace;
Don't think upon a woman, for your spouse,
Who's fond of visiting from house, to house:
For a good wife, will have no cause to roam,
She'll always find enough to do at home;
But in this town, some say, that you may find,
A certain idle class of women-kind;
Who rest not till their neighbour's faults are shown,
To all the town, but they forget their own:
Wherever they good entertainment find,
They often visit, and are very kind;
And some malicious people please to say,
They like to drink, but do not like to pay:
And those who can afford a drop of gin,
Are sure to have them after lying inn:
One comes and asks, how she the night did pass,
The bottle ready, she must have a glass:
Ah! what a pretty babe another cries,
It's daddy's picture, see its nose and eyes!
Thus they their precious moments idly squander,
But you, who do not wish from home to wander;
Pray do not think my satire, too severe,
The cap it is not meant for you to wear:

You women, who a gossipping have gone,
If the cap fits you, you may put it on:
  Go not 'mongst harlots, shun the fatal snare,
Flee from those stews, infections, come not there:
Nor wound your bodies, nor your soul debase,
Nor risk damnation for a snatch'd embrace.
A captain Stewart, that I knew right well,
Who left his wife, and went to a brothel;
Next day, his body was a shocking sight,
Half of it burnt; the house took fire that night;
This is a fact, well known at Billingsgate,
His brother there could prove what I relate.
Debauchery has such a frightful mein,
That to be hated, needs but to be seen.
Low and indelicate must be their taste,
Who in brothels their time and money waste;
Dead to those nobler passions, whence proceed
The lib'ral sentiment, and gen'rous deed:
For women higher let your love aspire,
Beyond the bounds of brutal base desire;
Friendship and love are pleasures more refin'd,
To those who taste the banquet of the mind,
Altho' with women I have spent much time,
A broken vow was never yet my crime;
That man who tries to gain the female heart,
Succeeds, then plays the worthless trifler's part;
And then makes game of all their sighs and tears,
And slights them, after courting them for years;
Does first their kindness and affection prove,
And then despises all he ought to love;
Boasting their weakness, then, his strength to show;
In mercy spare the base unmanly blow:
Who robs a woman of her peace of mind,

Should be despised by all female kind :
Altho' such men in worldly grandeur shine,
They never were companions of mine;
O, that each heart which female charms allure,
Were honest, gen'rous, undisguis'd and pure,
Ye sailors, don't deceive the innocent,
Nor talk of love without a pure intent,
But shun those jilts who of young men make game,
Yet try all arts your passions to inflame;
Who of their persons or their dress are proud,
Stares in men's faces and who laughs aloud;
Forbear to toy, or glance, or wishful gaze
Beneath the lawn which on the bosom plays;
Fine dress, and wanton gestures they display,
For which they make some foolish sailors pay :
Persuade to treat them both to play and ball—
Sailors are gen'rous they must pay for all;
Your money is their object all the while,
Until its spent deceive you with a smile;
But then despise the men by which they live;
Avoid them then, 'tis nobler far to give.
Let others take their girls and flowing bowls,
But let them see that you have nobler souls;
Let gratitude to God by works display
The obligations under which you lay:
And let the poor and wretched share a part;
Shew that a seaman has a feeling heart;
Consider those who are oblig'd to beg,
Instead of gold, have got a wooden leg;
Condemn'd to suffer scorn, neglect, disgrace,
Remember that it might have been your case,
They too for fortune's favours once did look,
But she has jilted them and quite forsook;

The only favour she bestow'd was this—
Marri'd them to her eldest daughter Miss.
One night I met a sailor sick and lame,
He could not speak, o'erpower'd with grief and shame
And modest diffidence his tongue withheld,
To put in practice what his wants compel'd.
Tho' silent, yet his looks they seem'd to say,
Shipmate afford me some relief, I pray,
I said, don't be offended, but I guess
You are in want, or else in some distress.
He bashfully reply'd, he was indeed,
And almost starv'd, but durst not tell his need.
Bursting in tears, he said, this two days past,
Believe me, sir, I have not broke my fast.
My cloaths are all in pawn, my bed also,
My wife is sick, and forc'd to lay on straw.
He said no more, because his eyes did see,
His flowing tears, had brought forth tears from me.
Not his, nor all men's tongues could more relate
Than I myself conceiv'd of his estate.
I thought I saw how sick his wife might lie,
And that I heard his half starv'd children cry,
And you who are to charity inclin'd,
Such objects of distress you oft will find;
That have not got their impudence of face,
Who idly beg their bread from place to place.
Then go amongst your neighbours round about,
And if you know of none, inquire them out.
Where meagre poverty with want opprest,
O'ercome with grief and ev'ry way distrest,
Heaves the big sigh, abandon'd to despair:
Give me a feeling heart, and send me there.
Let others sit in grandeur's costly seat,

I envy not the proud, the rich, the great.
To riches happiness is not confin'd,
For they can never ease a troubled mind:
When the world smiles on us the most of all,
We are in danger of the greatest fall;
The poor it seems are in the safest place,
But rich and poor may all be rich in grace.
   We see a Guinea ship sail round the rock,
The people run to see her come in dock;
The anchor's gone, she swings at the pier-head,
Some person hails, and asks, " How many's dead ?"
Of what went out, 'tis awful to reflect,
If half come back, they don't much more expect.
While looking round for faces that he knew,
The ship-keeper oft finds but very few:
O what a fatal this Guinea trade,
How many die, how few are sailors made !
Can christians join in such a trade as this !
'Tis not the way to gain eternal bliss:
The cruelties which they commit on board,
Will come to light when all shall be restor'd;
Of these poor negroes they again may hear,
When at the day of judgment all appear:
The man of pride, of insolence, and pow'r,
Who liv'd a tyrant to his dying hour;
Who dragg'd poor negroes from their native shore,
And by their suff'rings much increas'd his store;
How fain would he the day of judgment shun,
Give worlds of wealth if it could but be done;
But all in vain, he must his conduct own,
And then have judgment without mercy shown.
Then the poor slave no more his masters scoff,
Regains his freedom, flings his fetters off.

For worldly riches men their souls have sold,
Barter'd eternal life for cursed gold.
And still their crimes to nations yet unborn,
Remains on record to be read with scorn
Yes, they may love their pleasure and their pelf,
But can they love their neighbour as their self;
Too hard for them, therefore they never try,
To do to all as they would be done by.*
Who deal in slaves, they must have hearts like steel,
All tender hearts for suff'ring negroes feel,
Ye Britons, who of liberty can boast,
Are you become slave merchants on the coast?
You, who for liberty so boldly stand,
Shall this black traffic still disgrace your land ?
All Englishmen, who have a sense of shame,
Must feel indignant at the very name.
O may I always, while I hold my pen,
Feel for poor negroes as my fellow men ;
I've seen their suff'rings, and should I be dumb,
I might be punish'd in the world to come.

   I leave this trade, supported now by few,
And o'er the town I take another view ;

* In the year 1792, the town of Liverpool employed one hundred and thirty three ships, which carried to the West Indies thirty eight thousand nine hundred and twenty live slaves.—The English used to supply the West Indies with one hundred thousand Negroes every year; that is, so many were taken on board of their ships; but at least ten thousand of them died on the voyage; about a fourth part more died at the different islands, in what is called the seasoning. As to the punishments inflicted on them, says Sir Hans Sloane, they frequently geld them, or chop off half a foot; after they are whip'd till they are raw all over. Some put pepper and salt over them; some crop melted wax upon their skin; others cut off their ears and constrain them to broil and eat them for rebellion (that is asserting their native liberty, which they have as much right to as the air they breathe) they fasten them down to the ground with crooked sticks on every limb; and then applying fire by degrees to the feet and hands, they burn them gradually to the head. By the law of Barbadoes, if any Negro under punishment by his master or his order for running away, or any other crime, or misdemeanour, shall suffer in life or member, no person whatever shall be liable to any fine therefore. But if any man of wantonness, or only of bloody mindedness, or cruel intention, wilfully kill a Negro of his own, he shall pay into the public treasury fifteen pounds sterling; and not be liable to any other punishment or forfeiture for the same.
   *Thoughts upon Slavery, by.*
                   *JOHN WESLEY.*

Mount Pleasant Hill does a fine prospect shew,
There I can calmly view the town below;
Most men are busy how to get or spend,
Few of them think upon their latter end;
Some merchants they no leisure time can find,
But make excuse, they must their bus'ness mind;
For news-rooms, they neglect the church, and shew
Their mind is fix'd upon the things below;
And on a Sunday, if the day is fine,
Then they must in the country go to dine:
The worldly-minded, study to get rich,
And love of pleasure many doth bewitch;
Wealth makes the man, no matter how its got;
And riches wipes out ev'ry stain and blot.
Grown fat with wealth and ease, they oft despise
The very men by whom so high they rise;
Tho' from the poor, the labour of their bones,
The honey comes that feeds so many drones,
Amongst the poor are many wicked things,
Such as on cities swift destruction brings,
Perhaps some judgment yet may come upon
This very town, 'tis such a sinful one,
Amongst the rest, at this vast busy place,
A few are found who run the heav'nly race;
Some happy souls are in this town who prove,
That their new heart are fix'd on things above:
Some who were slaves to sin, but now, behold,
They grow in grace, as they in years grow old;
Ah, what a change! the sinner now relents;
And of his sins, sincerely he repents;
All stand astonish'd when they do him view,
" Is this the man," they say, " whom once we knew?
" The man who once sang madly, danc'd and laugh'd,

" And drunk in dizzy madness with his draught,
" Has wept a silent flood, revers'd his ways,
" Is sober, chaste, benevolent, and prays;
He knows that Jesus bought him with his blood,
And bold he stands confess'd a child of God.
Such striking wonders of redeeming grace,
Have many times been witness'd in this place.

May all who are preserv'd upon the deep,*
These mercies still in their remembrance keep;
And when on shore tell of his wond'rous ways,
And let your joyful songs be songs of praise:
And you who oft did blast your eyes and limbs,
Now worship God in singing psalms and hymns;
The judgments which you did on others call,
Pray that on your own heads they may not fall:
'Tis strange that men, so much indulg'd by Heav'n,
To swearing should habitually be giv'n;
He who preserves you on the wat'ry main,
Dare you still take his sacred name in vain!
Can blasphemy, which must your souls o'erwhelm,
Assist to work the ship, or guide the helm?
While deeds unmatch'd your dauntless courage tell,
Forbear to use this dialect of hell:
" Maintain your rank, vulgarity despise,
" To swear is neither brave, polite, nor wise."

* Sailors who have escaped so many dangers, have peculiar obligations lying
on them to praise God for the wonderful preservations they have experienced,
may they see and consider frequently and seriously the alarming situations
they have been in; the horrors their minds have felt on the occasion; the ear-
nest prayers they put up to God for help; and the many solemn vows then
made to devote their spared life to him! the awful apprehension of the body
sinking into the sea, and the soul launching into the ocean of eternity, in all
the impurity of sin, guilty and condemned, is enough to strike speechless the
boldest seaman that ever sailed in a ship. You who have followed the sea
twenty, thirty, or forty years, you have taken many a painful farewel of your
friends and families; you have been in the utmost peril, when you thought that
you should never meet your friends again But O! the wonderful goodness of
God! he has preserved and brought you safe to port, this is the Lord's doing, and
it is marvellous in our eyes.

## THE END.

# EXPERIENCE,

WHILE safe at home you landsmen keep,
Remember those who plow the deep,
 And leave their friends and ease ;
We social pleasures must not share,
Watching at night, the ship's our care,
 To guide across the seas.

How oft the Lord did call to me,
In danger both on land and sea,
 And warn'd from sin to part;
He try'd me with prosperity,
And likewise by adversity :
 These did not change my heart.

When fortune smil'd, and fill'd my breast
With dreams of creature happiness,
 This seem'd a pleasant road ;
More I enjoy'd of worldly wealth,
Of friends, of pleasure, and of health,
 The more I ran from God.

I oft repented when alone,
But by companions hurried on,
 Was driven with the stream ;
Till God his chast'ning rod did shake :
Affliction caus'd me to awake
 Out of this golden dream.

When death it star'd me in the face,
I saw that hell must be my place,
  I was not fit to die;
I promis'd, if my life was spar'd,
That I would strive to be prepar'd,
  And from temptations fly.

In my own strength I vainly strove,
But wanting wisdom from above,
  I could not conquer sin;
Tho' outwardly I sin did shun,
Yet from myself I could not run,
  I felt it dwell within.

No happincs I then could find,
But horrid thoughts possess'd my mind,
  Which brought me near despair;
I read the Bible, try'd to pray,
But yet was fearful all the way,
  God would not hear my prayer.

For then I thought it was too late,
That I must be a reprobate,
  And into hell be cast;
My sins all star'd me in the face,
Said I deserv'd no other place,
  My days of grace was past.

" Alas !" I cri'd, " where shall I go,
" I have done all that I can do,
  " But can't from sin get free :'"
Then I society did shun,
And thought no man beneath the sun,
  Was half so bad as me.

When far from home wand'ring about,
There the good shepherd found me out—
　　Brought back against my will;
He would not let the captive go,
I found no resting place below,
　　His love pursu'd me still.

How clear the love of God did show,
Let by a way I did not know,
　　Where he design'd to bless;
When most I felt the want of grace,
Then Jesus shew'd his smiling face,
　　And to my soul spoke peace.

My happy soul now soars above
All earthly and all creature love,
　　Now by the Son made free;
In God alone I sweetly rest,
I lean upon my Saviour's breast,
　　He's all in all to me.

I go to sea at his command,
And tell when I come on the land,
　　The wonders of his love;
Now safe in Christ, the ark, I sail,
I know his promise will not fail,
　　But land me safe above,

*FINIS.*

———

*G. Wilson Printer, Leeds.*

www.ingramcontent.com/pod-product-compliance
Lightning Source LLC
Chambersburg PA
CBHW081522040426
42447CB00013B/3303